ECHOES OF WAR

Although the guns were silent over the fields and hills of Europe, they still rumbled in my head. . . .

Dark memories still shuffled in kaleidoscopic confusion: images of death and destruction; mutilations of mind and body, bewilderingly highlighted here and there by flickers of compassion, tenderness, and even love.

It seemed possible that a return to those times and places might help me make sense (if sense could be made) of what had taken place. Might help to mute or even still the echoes of those guns.

By Farley Mowat

FARLEY MOWAT

Aftermath

Travels in a Post-War World

SEAL BOOKS
McClelland-Bantam, Inc. • Toronto

This edition contains the complete text
of the original hardcover edition.
NOT ONE WORD HAS BEEN OMITTED.

AFTERMATH
A Seal Book / published by arrangement with
Key Porter Books Limited.

PUBLISHING HISTORY
Key Porter edition published in 1995
Seal edition / September 1996

CIP: 95-931872-0
All rights reserved.
Copyright © 1995 by Farley Mowat.
Cover photograph courtesy of the author.
No part of this book may be reproduced or transmitted in any form
or by any means, electronic or mechanical, including photocopying,
recording, or by any information storage and retrieval system,
without permission in writing from the publisher.

For information address:
Key Porter Books Limited
70 The Esplanade
Toronto, Ontario
Canada M5E 1R2

ISBN 0-770-42726-X

Seal Books are published by McClelland-Bantam, Inc. Its trademark,
consisting of the words "Seal Books" and the portrayal of a seal, is
the property of McClelland-Bantam, Inc., 105 Bond Street, Toronto,
Ontario M5B 1Y3, Canada. This trademark has been duly registered
in the Trademark Office of Canada. The trademark consisting of the
words "Bantam Books" and the portrayal of a rooster is the property
of and is used with the consent of Bantam Books, 1540 Broadway,
New York, New York 10036. This trademark has been duly registered
in the Trademark Office of Canada and elsewhere.

PRINTED IN CANADA

UNI 0 9 8 7 6 5 4 3 2 1

GLIMPSES OF A WORLD THAT WAS.

FOR KIMBERLY AND ROBERT 'SANDY' MOWAT.

Contents

Foreword

It is in our nature to travel into our past, hoping thereby to illuminate the darkness that bedevils the present. And it is in the nature of things that we can seldom manage, in that fine old phrase, to part the veils of time.

Hitler's war ended in May of 1945. On several occasions during the next half century, I revisited the scenes that had loomed large for me in that war, but only once did I come close to overleaping time and penetrating the obscurity.

I do not know why this one particular excursion should have been more successful than the others. I can only suppose the circumstances must have been singularly appropriate or else that the custodians of time past happened to let down their guard.

War's end had found me in western Europe, where I remained until the end of 1945, serving as a kind of glorified garbage man, charged with collecting samples of the weaponry that had obliterated some thirty or forty million human beings.

By the time I returned to Canada I desperately wished to escape from what had been, and seemed likely to remain, a world run by maniacs. So I fled north to spend much of 1947 on the tundra plains of Keewatin, northwest of Churchill. There I lived and travelled with a young Métis, who introduced me to the barrenland caribou, arctic wolves, and a little-known and dwindling tribe of inland-dwelling Inuit. This powerful experience drew me back the following year in the guise of a field biologist employed by the federal government to study the interaction of wolves and caribou.

During the ensuing ten months I observed wolves and caribou but also became deeply involved in trying to halt the dissolution overtaking the inland Inuit. My employers concluded that, in so doing, I was exceeding the terms of my employment. While Frances, my wife of a year, and I were wintering in a native village, I was fired.

We two returned south in February of 1949 and for the rest of that year I put in time at a university. The following spring we bought ten acres of swamp forty miles northwest of Toronto and we set about building a base from which I could pursue the writing profession.

By first snow in the autumn of 1950 we had constructed a log home big enough to house the two of us and a husky dog. Just before Christmas I sold a short story about the inland Inuit, and early in 1951 the editors of *Atlantic Monthly* asked me to write a book about those beleaguered people.

Publication of *People of the Deer* in 1952 stimulated the Hastings and Prince Edward Regiment, with which both my father and I had served during the war, to ask if I would accept a commission to write a regimental history.

I was reluctant. Although the guns were silent over the fields and hills of Europe, they still rumbled in my head, giving rise to a bedlam of grotesqueries where nothing was as it might seem or ought to be. Dark memories still shuffled in kaleidoscopic confusion: images of death and destruction; mutilations of mind and body, bewilderingly highlighted here and there by flickers of compassion, tenderness, and even love.

However, the more I thought about the offer, the more it seemed possible that a return to those times and places might help me make sense (if sense could be made) of what had taken place. Might help to mute or even still the echoes of the guns.

There was another thing. Although I had spent three wartime years in Britain, Italy, France, and the Low Countries, almost everything I had seen or experienced had been distorted by the overtones of war. The real lives of the inhabitants and the real nature of the lands our heavy boots had marched across had evaded me. Perhaps, I thought, if I went back I could discover something of what I had missed.

So I agreed to write the book; and was rewarded by what was then a truly munificent advance — three thousand dollars!

With the cheque before us, Fran and I reviewed our situation. Conventional wisdom suggested we invest the bulk of the money and use the interest to pay our daily bills. On the other hand, we had no debts and were beholden to nobody.

We were growing much of our own food and cutting our own fuel in our own woods. And we were both confident (Fran more so than I) that I could keep the bailiff from the door by writing short stories and articles.

These things having been duly and soberly discussed, we decided to blow the whole three grand. Sixteen hundred of it would go to purchasing a Hillman Minx convertible, which we would take delivery of in England. The rest would pay the shot for a voyage of exploration that would last as long as the money did. And, instead of booking a slow, but economical, passage by ship, we would overleap the Atlantic by air, and hang the cost.

Reaction from friends and relatives ranged from the appalled conclusion that we had gone out of our minds to stern admonitions about the importance of maintaining financial probity. We did, however, have the positive support of some old friends, including Andy Lawrie, companion of my youth, who would be house-sitting and husky-walking during our absence.

"Listen, kids," he told us, "one way or the other, the long claw of the Sea Puss is going to get us all in the end. So give him a run for the money!"

To London Town

TRANS-CANADA Airlines' North Star, a refurbished wartime DC-4, departed from Malton airport north of Toronto in a drizzle on the first day of May.

Fran had never before been in an aeroplane and I had never been in such a large one, so we unabashedly held hands as we stared uneasily out the small porthole into the swirling murk. We were not blessed with the *savoir-faire* of the other passengers, mainly members of southern Ontario's business élite bound for England to make their contributions to the festivities attendant on the Coronation of Queen Elizabeth the Second. They exuded confidence and we marvelled at them.

As the aircraft lumbered along at seventeen thousand feet, we were given trays of chicken salad and tomato aspic, which we had to balance precariously on pillows held on our laps, but we did have real silver, linen napkins, and crystal wine glasses.

The wine did Fran a lot of good.

"If we have to go down in flames," she said, with a side-long glance out the porthole at the red-hot exhaust of the nearest Merlin engine, "at least we'll go in style."

"Yes," I assured her, "and in good company. I'll bet there isn't a passenger on the plane, except us, making less than fifty thou a year."

"Then we won't let on about you being a socialist," said she, settling back with a Raymond Chandler thriller.

We descended into Goose Bay, Labrador, an hour before dusk, landing at a nominally Canadian, but effectively American, air force base. While the plane was being refuelled, we were herded into a bleak hangar by an armed escort. The task of our slouching and slovenly guards was to prevent the Russian spies amongst us from taking pictures of Sabre jets and antique bombers parked in the dim distance. Our fellow passengers were titillated and, it may be, reassured by this evidence that the defenders of capitalism were on their toes.

Darkness had fallen before we ascended for the twenty-three-hundred-mile, ten-hour voyage across the ocean. Our seats were beside the starboard wing, and one of the Rolls-Royce Merlins was only an arm's length away. Its manifold glowed threateningly, while the outboard engine spat a long stream of blue flame. The bellowing thunder kept us from sleep. We squirmed stickily in our seats the long night through, and got no good of it.

The morning of a sunny spring day had dawned when we regained the land, making a lazy swing over the green islands of Arran and Kintyre before descending into a Royal Air Force base at Prestwick. The air was warm and soft and flowers ringed the shabby, wartime buildings. There were no armed guards here — only a family of young jackdaws perched on a roof ridge, nerving themselves for first flight. Whenever an aircraft roared off the runway, they would teeter forward yearningly then, at the last moment, lose their nerve and scrabble back up the ridge pole.

Airborne again, we flew south at comparatively low altitude, avidly taking in the sights. Great numbers of small, round ponds scattered in fields and woods near Liverpool piqued Fran's curiosity. What could they be?

"Bomb craters," I told her. "German bombs which missed Liverpool or were jettisoned by Jerry pilots anxious to head for home. Look at them now! Pretty little frog ponds for cows to drink out of and kids to paddle in."

At London airport, we boarded a bus for the long ride into the city. A lanky, well-dressed fellow carrying a cowboy hat on his lap shared the seat in front of us with a pock-marked woman possessed of a high-pitched and penetrating voice, which she took no pains to modulate. We soon learned they were brother and sister who had not seen each other since he had emigrated to Canada thirty years earlier. He was trying to maintain and stimulate the high excitement of homecoming. She was doing her determined best to damp him down.

First, she gave him hell for landing at London airport instead of Croydon, which would have been "so much more convenient for *us*. But then, you never did think of anyone else's convenience, did you?" She gave him hell for having stayed away so long: "We could all have died of old age or been blown up by Hitler's gang for what you cared!" She chewed on his Canadian accent for a while, then had a go at his Stetson: "What a silly thing for a grown man to wear. But it don't surprise me. Wouldn't surprise me if you'd brought along a Red Indian squaw as well."

Our stop came before his and as I passed his seat I could not help asking sympathetically, "You get your rabies shot before you left home, chum? Looks as if you might need it."

Fran dragged me away before I could hear his rejoinder — if there was one.

A taxi dropped us at our hotel. I had instructed a Toronto travel agency to book us into a modest hostelry. Instead, we found ourselves guests of the Green Park Hotel, which, if not the swankiest of the swank, was close enough to discomfit me. Dirty and dishevelled, we slunk up to a luxurious room behind a phalanx of bellhops. I hated to think what the bill was going to be, but there was some compensation: Fran was so pleased with her new quarters, she forgave me the incident in the bus.

Next day was Sunday and, there being nothing we could do to advance our journey, we decided to become trippers. London was already full of tourists enjoying the balmy spring weather. I led Fran down the Mall so I could show her what London looked like, but the Old Lady was so heavily bedraped and bedecked with webs of scaffolding, miles of bunting, and forests of flags that we could hardly get a peek at her face.

"Coronation's going to be quite a show," I said.

Fran's reply was a bit wistful. "It's too bad we have to miss it. We *do* have to miss it, don't we?"

"No choice. All our bookings are made and can't be changed at this late date." I did not tell her, then or later, how carefully I had planned things to ensure we would be far from Britain before Coronation mania reached its peak. Not that I am anti-monarchist. My problem was, and is, that the spectacle of human beings aggregating like swarming bees sounds a tocsin somewhere in my deep subconscious. I know there is a point of critical mass that, if reached, will unleash the lemming syndrome and send the multitudes pouring helter-skelter into the nearest body of water. I just didn't want to be in London when it happened.

If not much else was visible, St. Paul's was still able to elevate its dome above the tinsel. I flagged a cab to take us there. When the driver heard I had been in London during the Blitz, he volunteered a guided tour of the bombed-out wastelands behind the cathedral. The spectacle of those endless blocks of rubble was a stunner for Frances.

"I could never have believed the bombing was that bad. How did anyone survive?"

"Few would have if the Nazis had been able to do what they intended. The idea was to blow and burn London right off the map. Show us what Total War really meant. Knock Britain to her knees. Just good luck, the RAF, and Goering's stupidities prevented the whole city being reduced to slag."

"Aye," said our driver, "they bastards'd have buried us. And yet there's folks from your side of the water thinks we ought to feel guilty-like for what we done to German cities when we got the upper hand. Guilty!" he spat out the cab window. "Cor! When I hears that from a fare, I brings him here, whether he likes or no."

Though the ruins were ten years old, little had been done to clean up the mess. This was because, our driver explained, the land was so valuable it could not find buyers.

"Never you mind about that, though. The grass has come back, and the flowers, and the trees and, if we leave it to that lot and the birds and the beasts, they'll do a proper clean-up job."

We toured the cathedral. By then it was time for a pint and a sausage roll in a nearby pub before tackling the Tower, which was high on Fran's obligatory list. It seethed with visitors. We walked the old stones, viewing jewels, Cockneys, cannon, Beefeaters, dungeons, Bostonians, old armour, Torontonians, et al., until I'd had a surfeit.

My attention strayed to the Tower ravens. One old fellow was standing in the middle of a bit of greensward amusing himself with what looked suspiciously like a conscious imitation of us tourists. He would peer incredulously at some fragment of brick or stone, then shriek his astonishment to a circle of fellow ravens. Now and then he would cast a gleeful look at passing humans and give a raucous whoop of derision. I tipped him a conspiratorial wink.

We boarded a boat at Tower Landing and went homeward on the river where, Sunday or no, London was at work. Barge traffic was heavy and there was no Coronation frippery about the trim ocean-going freighters unloading at rows of ramshackle riverside storehouses left gap-toothed by losses sustained during the bombings.

Cutting back across Green Park to our hotel, we encountered half of London lounging about in deck chairs, sprawled on plaid rugs, or strolling amongst the trees like so many villagers. There were nearly as many dogs as people and the dogs, at least, showed little of the fabled British reserve. Fran was accosted by a lecherous Great Dane who was inclined to treat me as a competitor. We were rescued by an apologetic gentleman in flannels with binoculars slung around his neck.

"Dreadfully sorry," he murmured. "Fact is, old Roger here seems to have spring fever."

We chatted for a while about dogs, and the birds on the ponds. When I remarked that London's parks were her saving grace, I rather expected a defensive reply. But no.

"Quite right, old boy. They make it liveable, if barely so. We'd be wise to turn the bombed-out patches into new parks. Places for people to breathe. But we shan't, shall we? Too many quid to be made out of piling up the bricks and stone again." He shrugged, whistled to Roger, and departed.

I lay awake for a while that night, thinking about the Tower ravens; the myriad coots, ducks, geese, and swans on the park ponds; the house sparrows, starlings, and pigeons in the squares; and about something else our knowledgeable taxi driver had told us. Foxes, stoats, weasels, hedgehogs, rabbits, and pheasants had all begun colonizing the urban wastelands produced by the bombing. "It's old Mother Nature taking back her own," he'd said. Nurturing that consoling thought I drifted off to sleep.

———————————————

I woke Monday morning dreading the prospects, for on this day we would cease to be carefree tourists and acquire a car — together with all the problems that inevitably accompany the automotive incubus.

We went first to the city showroom of the Rootes Group (which looked and felt like a bank) and were properly subdued by the frock-coated magnificence and hauteur of the staff. They were kind but distant, as befitted gentlemen's gentlemen dedicated to the service of Aston Martins and Sunbeam Talbots. I got the impression that Hillmans were definitely below the salt, and so were we. Nevertheless, after much signing of papers written in ancient English legalese, we were dispatched to the Rootes garage, there to take delivery of a spanking-new, claret-coloured Minx convertible whom we immediately named Elizabeth in honour of the young queen. Liz was the first real car (war-surplus jeeps excepted) we had ever owned, and very sporty she looked with her top neatly furled. I started her up, and we were off.

The Queen's Brew

MOUNTING the North Downs we made our way out of London into Kent, where roadside gorse flared daffodil-yellow. The smoke haze of the city soon gave way to a translucent haze of sea air drifting inland from the distant Channel. For an hour we ambled along while I tried to get the feel of driving on the left of the road, and Liz got the feel of me at the helm. We had no choice but to drive slowly, being under orders to stay below thirty-five miles per hour during a "break-in" run of five hundred miles.

Reaching the valley of the Daren River, we descended into the little town of Westerham. Here we were seduced by the rococo magnificence of the King's Arms hotel. We parked Liz, entered the inn, and asked the barman for two pints of mild. Before he could draw them, a smallish man with moist brown eyes and a ruddy complexion spoke up from his spot near the bar.

"Make that two Coronations, George."

George set two full glasses before us with a word of apology.

"You mustn't mind Freddie here. He makes this ruddy stuff and he's dotty about it."

We thanked the little man and praised the brew, which *was* extraordinary. And that was how we fell into Freddie Holden's toils.

Freddie, who was about my age, did not talk much about himself, but I later learned he had been born and raised in a country public house in Gloucestershire. He had enlisted in the army in 1940 and served as a tank driver through the North African and Italian campaigns, during which, although three tanks were "shot out from under him," he escaped serious injury.

"What kept me going was a plan I had. When I was not much more than a nipper, I made up me mind to be a master brewer, and I never give up on that. If anything, the war and the desert made me more determined. Dry work out there, you know. When I was demobbed in '45, I set about making it come right."

In 1946, in answer to an advertisement for an apprentice, he came down to the Black Eagle Brewery in Westerham, was accepted, and served a three-year "pupillage," as it is called in the trade. Then he went up to London for "advanced studies" in the plants of the huge Meux brewery empire. While there he took time off to slip back to Gloucestershire and marry the girl who had been waiting for him since 1940.

"Couldn't see me way clear to doing it before. Wouldn't have done, you know, to start a family till I could look after them proper-like. But Peggy and me has made up for the delay. Three nippers in four years. By the last of them I was back in Westerham. Now I'm assistant brew master and one day, God willing, may be the master."

I don't quite know why Freddie should have taken such a shine to us. Perhaps because he and I had both served in Italy. Perhaps he was a little enamoured of Frances. Probably, though, it was the missionary in him. In any case, nothing would do but that we stay over in Westerham and allow him to induct us into the mystic order of British brewers that very evening.

"I'll be by for you at eight o'clock sharp, after you've had your bite of dinner," he told us. "The lads'll have gone home from Black Eagle by then and the works'll be quiet. Night's the best time there. 'Tis then you feel what you might call the spirit of the place."

I doubt that he was punning.

Promptly at eight he met us in the saloon bar and led us out into quiet streets. We followed him down a steeply sloping lane until we stood before the shadowy Victorian façade of

Black Eagle, one of the last of a diminishing handful of small, independent British breweries and one of the oldest.

"Folk hardly know when it begun. Black Eagle's name's been on to it since the eighteenth century but there was a brewery here long afore that." Freddie gave us a quizzical smile. "I sometimes wonder, wasn't it always here?"

He opened the great oaken doors with an iron key the size of his hand. Once we were inside, the Victorian image was revealed as a thin veneer grafted onto an ancient past. By the light of an electric torch we moved back in time. Wooden floors gave way to flagstones under low, timbered ceilings. The warm and vital odour of living yeast flowed through stone-arched corridors like a tangible presence, drawing us deeper and deeper into antiquity.

Freddie guided us first into a stone-walled room floored with hand-hewn planks and almost full of fat burlap sacks of malt.

Most malting barley, Freddie told us, was grown in Yorkshire and Norfolk by farmers who had been at it for generations. The best could be raised only on fields manured by sheep. During the war, when sheep became scarce, the quality of the barley dropped appreciably. "Warn't fit for porridge, let alone ale," was Freddie's opinion. Commercial fertilizers would not serve as a substitute. Sheep it had to be.

Farmers sent one-pound samples of their crop to the breweries. Black Eagle got fifty or sixty such each autumn. Each received an evaluation which owed little to science and much to instinct. Although an old brass microscope stood in the sampling room, it was seldom used. The master brewer, seventy-three-year-old William Wickett, made his preliminary selection based on the colour, weight, and feel of the grain. Then some of each chosen batch was ground into flour for Wickett and Freddie to taste — and argue about. The ultimate decision rested with Wickett, who had been brewing since his fifteenth birthday and was the son and grandson of Black Eagle master brewers.

"'Twould be his own son standing here now, 'stead of me," Freddie told us, "only the poor fellow was killed when our chaps had to pull out at Dunkirk. Terrible bad luck. I could wish for William's sake it'd been otherwise."

The chosen barley went to Black Eagle's maltster, who plied his trade in the shadow of a stone kiln in the brewery yard.

The barley starch was inert and insoluble until the maltster tricked the barley germ into performing a miracle for him. Having steeped the grain in warm water for fifty hours, he spread it on the uneven stone floor of the malt house. Embryo cells then began to stir, multiply, and secrete an enzyme that slowly converted the starch to sugar. The process took ten days, after which, having served the maltster's purpose, the embryos perished in the heat of the kiln.

Kilning, we learned, is the most demanding part of the maltster's art. Several kinds of malt were required at Black

Eagle, and each had to be perfectly baked, else the age-old flavour of the brew would suffer. Malt for bitter ales was cooked to a light golden colour; for mild ales to a rich mahogany; for stouts, chocolate coloured.

"The malt has to be just right — but so does the water," Freddie told us. "Not too hard. Not too soft. Most water is good for nowt but washing up."

"Couldn't you regulate the hardness by adding or subtracting salts?" I asked, attempting to sound knowledgeable.

Freddie looked pained. "Oh, aye, that can be done. But if there's breweries as'll tamper with the liquor — that's what we call the water used to make the brew — we be not among them. Good ale, you see, has got to be natural, like mother's milk. Made by God's own living creatures — the barley germ and the yeast. Our job is mainly just to keep an eye peeled so nothing goes wrong. If you speaks of adding things, you're not talking about Black Eagle."

According to Freddie, only a few score water sources in Britain were "just right." And one of the best was in Westerham. There is presumptive evidence that people were brewing here in prehistoric times, using surface springs. But over the millennia the water table sank and now Black Eagle's supply came from three hundred feet down — crystalline, bitterly cold and slightly alkaline. The springs were earmarked for emergency use in case a catastrophe left London without sufficient drinking water. Great iron hydrants capped with embossed leaden seals, not to be broken except in case of dire emergency, ringed the brewery like sentinels.

Freddie showed us where malted barley was shovelled into a hopper in the malt room floor. A wooden chute worn thin by centuries of use carried the grain two floors down to an ancient, cast-iron grinder, where it was pulverized. The resulting sandy-looking substance then descended yet another level to be deposited in an iron drum called the mash tun. Here hot water dissolved the sugars out of the malted grain.

We followed Freddie down through a dim-lit maze of pipes and twisting corridors, then up steep stone stairs to the brewery's top floor. Here, in its own great room under a high-arched roof, stood the copper — a vast, rotund, polished vessel, into whose belly the mixture of liquor and malt — now known as the wort — was pumped from four floors down.

Freddie's enthusiasm mounted as we penetrated farther into the works. He was almost trotting as he led us along to the hop room, which was filled nearly to its high ceiling with enormous, cloth-wrapped bales. Fran and I found ourselves gasping for breath, so pungent was the resinous scent.

"These are the best hops to be had anywhere," Freddie declared. "Grown here in Kent. Nothing like them."

Traditionally, Kentish hops had been gathered by people from London's slums, and campgrounds used by pickers through the centuries were still to be found scattered throughout the hop-growing region.

"One time," said Freddie, "I saw four generations of Cockneys picking together. There was a great-grandmother filling her big wicker basket alongside of her own great-granddaughter. It were a late-summer holiday them times, a festival you might call it, that Londoners looked forward to. Pretty well finished now. Them new hop-picking machines is elbowing out the folk as still comes down. But Black Eagle won't touch hops picked by a machine! Nor ever will, if I has any say on it."

Hops were dried at the farms, whose ancient, high-pointed stone kilns remain a feature of the Kentish landscape.

Pulverized hop cones were added to the wort in the great copper, Freddie told us, after which the round door was bolted shut and live steam piped in. Two hours later the liquid — now called hop wort — was drawn off into the hop back, an immense wooden vessel one floor down, where the residues were allowed to settle out.

Finally the clarified hop wort descended into the brewing hall, where the yeast was added. Black Eagle's long, dark hall housed fifteen copper-lined, wooden vats — squares as they are called in the trade — holding from nine hundred to seven thousand gallons each. Freddie told us that one or more squares always contained a working brew. "As long as Black Eagle's been here and, I don't doubt, a good many hundred year before that, it was thought the worst kind of luck not to *always* have a brew on the go. 'Twould be like breaking a link in a chain that goes so far back nobody knows where it began."

Nobody knows the origin or age of Black Eagle's yeast strain, either. Untold billions of cells have lived and died in the squares, and perhaps the strain has evolved into a distinct life form peculiar to Black Eagle. Caring for the yeast was Freddie's special responsibility, and he was as assiduous about it as any nursing mother about her offspring. Several times a day, he stared through his old microscope at samples, anxiously alert for any sign of sickness or of failing energy in his minute charges.

Resting yeast (partially dried and resembling soft white cheese fluffed up a bit) was kept in a cold-room in the deepest cellar. When added to the warm hop wort, the hungry cells would rouse from their lethargy and soon send a vanilla-coloured foam of ferment billowing up the sides of the square.

On the third day most of the foam was drawn off and put to rest again. On the eleventh day, the brew itself was decanted from the square, piped down into the cellars, and racked in casks.

We descended flights of worn stone stairs to the holy of holies — the dark, dank, and musty-smelling caverns where the brews matured. Old brick arches hemmed us in. Ranged between them were rows of casks, handmade of Polish oak by a cooper and his apprentice in a shed in the brewery yard. Freddie pointed the beam of his torch at the different sizes: pins, holding four gallons; firkins, holding nine; kilderkins, eighteen; twenty-gallon barrels; and fat hogsheads, holding fifty.

The bulk of Black Eagle's products were shipped after three weeks' maturation, he told us.

"Those are green brews, though. We hold some in wood for months before bottling. But what's the good of talk when you can taste? Come along wi' me."

Freddie took us to the tasting room, a whitewashed stone crypt, where he lovingly introduced us to each of the eleven brews made at Black Eagle. We began with plebian draft ales — bitter, mild, stout, and old — then switched to bottles and sloshed our way through brown, pale, and winter, concluding, and none too soon, with audit ale.

According to Freddie, only three British breweries still made audit ale, which was matured in casks for one month then in bottles for nine, and had an unarguable authority.

"The monks made it in old King Hal's time," Freddie told us. "Every year when the king's tax collectors came around to audit the monastery records, the canny old boogers would fill them up on audit ale until they couldn't add or subtract and hardly knew their own names."

Freddie was particularly proud of the special ale, brewed for Elizabeth II's coronation. It had lain in casks for six months, then matured four more in bottles stored in the darkest, coolest corner of the cellars. Smoky and as smooth as mellow wine, it was nearly as potent as malt whisky.

"There's been a royal ale brewed special for the coronation of every king and queen since George III, if not before. I've myself got bottles from four reigns that I'll hand on to me own lads to hand on down the line. Drink them? Why, I'd as soon stick a 1830 threepenny blue stamp on a letter!"

It was well after midnight before Fran and I came away from the Black Eagle, each clutching an unopened bottle of coronation ale — the Queen's Brew, as Freddie called it. We had solemnly assured him, and each other, we would never open them.

Both bottles burst inside our suitcases in the unpressurized luggage hold of the North Star that flew us back to Canada. But the aroma remained for a long time to remind us of the Queen's Brew, and of Freddie Holden.

Gaie Paris

WE made a somewhat bleary-eyed start next day, driving out of Westerham along a sunken road through a green-velvet valley. Just for the hell of it, we stopped at Chartwell, Winston Churchill's home. A courteous bobby at the gate informed us that Winston was not receiving, but made amiable conversation about the birds singing in the nearby hedgerows on this fine May day.

Although I was getting the hang of keeping to the left in a left-hand-drive car, I preferred to stay on minor roads, and we were well rewarded for doing so. The lanes of Kent were vivid with gorse flowering along the roadsides and on the heaths; bluebells grass-thick everywhere; and masses of once-cultivated flowers, now gone astray, having their ways with bees in the ditches.

Winding southward, we came off the Downs, crossed the serendipitously named Eden River and traversed Ashdown Forest; which was no forest at all, but a broad and rolling moor with a few gaunt pines straggling on distant hills. A kite soared overhead and robins of the English sort scuffled amidst the bracken.

Surrey now lay before us under a delicate haze that accentuated the perfection of the morning. We paused to pass the time of day with a postman on his bicycle; a farmer trimming his roadside hedgerows; a bevy of sheep claiming the right of way; and a tweedy lady with field glasses who waved us down, demanding in peremptory fashion if we had seen the corncrake.

"It's been heard in the neighbourhood," she said enthusiastically. "The first in twenty years. If you should spot it, do let me know." With which she scrambled through a break in a hedge and vanished.

"Alice in Wonderland country," said Fran, a bit bemusedly.

So we came to the hamlet of Blackboys and to nearby Possingworth Park. The great mansion within the gates appeared deserted, except for a gardener who may have been deaf, since he did not even look up as Liz scrunched the gravel in the circular drive.

Here, ten years earlier, the Hastings and Prince Edward Regiment had lived through a long wet winter under canvas or in metal Nissen huts. No indications of our erstwhile presence now remained.

For Fran's benefit, I recalled being on duty as orderly officer one wild December night. Rain and sleet beating on the tin roof of the hut almost drowned out the discordant mutter of enemy bombers high overhead. The door was flung open and a sodden, wild-eyed sentry burst in.

"Fuckin' parachutists!" he bellowed. "Comin' right down on top of us! Call out the fuckin' guard!"

If this was an invasion, I was the man to deal with it. Not only did I call out the guard, I put the entire battalion on stand-to, then alerted brigade headquarters. By the time the colonel got to the orderly room, several hundred half-naked, half-armed soldiers were milling around in the mud and rain like aimless water buffaloes. The telephone exchange was ringing like a banshee.

"Oh, my God, Mowat," said my commanding officer. "What the hell have you done *now*?"

"What *had* you done, Farley?" Fran asked sweetly.

"I'd made a slight mistake, that's all. It turned out the invader — there was only one — was a dud two-thousand-pound land mine of the sort the Germans liked to drop by parachute to achieve maximum blast effect. Had it detonated, it wouldn't have created half the fuss that resulted from my attempt to deal with a perceived invasion. Of course, come to think of it, there wouldn't have been anybody left around to raise a fuss if it *had* gone off."

"What happened to the bomb?"

"Oh, some scruffy-looking Limey from a bomb disposal squad, with a George Cross in his pocket and a screwdriver in his hand, came along and disarmed the thing, and they hauled it away. The colonel got the parachute and gave it to his girlfriend for dress goods. Me? Well, I got — if you'll pardon the phrase — shit from on high."

We drove back to Blackboys to see about lunch at a little pub I had once frequented. It was now in the hands of a pretentious, middle-aged London couple who had gussied it up with horse brasses and hunting prints. They offered a casual menu of scraps. During the meal the place was invaded by a party of city folk, including a Decayed Brigadier, a Bright Young Thing, a City Man, and a World-Weary Socialite. They were friendly in the vague way of their kind, but I missed the company of the local farmers and Land Army girls who had used the pub in other times.

We drove on to Waldron village, once home to our regimental headquarters. The Waldron pub was unchanged: small, dark, and long-lived-in. I identified myself to the publican. He did not remember me but did recollect the time the Regiment got a new CO who insisted that all officers do an hour's physical training in the village square before breakfast. In consequence, such portly figures as our paymaster, quartermaster, and adjutant, who were not built for such absurdities, made an indelible mark on the local scene.

"Folks used to come from miles around to see the show,"

the publican chuckled. "Aye, we were glad enough to have you Canucks here then . . . but o'course we was just as glad when you all went away."

I thought about how insignificant our stay here had been as Fran and I walked across the road to the parish church. There is none lovelier in all England. It overlooks the rich valley of Wallsend Water. The sweep of mossy verdancy that falls gently away from it is an Elysian field, dotted with spinneys of chestnut and oak and companionable clots of fat cattle.

The churchyard was small and wild, full of flowers that were no man's care. It seemed we had the world to ourselves for, in all the valley, no human being stirred. Passing through the old lych-gate, we let ourselves into the shadowed coolness of the church. A brass plaque listed the rectors. They began with one, Harold, in the year 1070. Harold had no title and, apparently, no surname, but was remembered nonetheless.

It was the devil to have to hurry on, but we had a date with the cross-Channel ferry next morning. We drove southward to Hailsham, then east along the coast to Winchelsea, where we stopped for tea at a little shop in the shadow of a hop kiln.

Tea is the redemption of English culinary arts, which, for the most part, are god-awful. For two shillings each, we had pots of Darjeeling, homemade bread, slathers of Devonshire cream, four kinds of homemade jam, hot buttered biscuits, and a variety of fruit and honey cakes. We thought that the provident tourist in England would do well to have tea three or four times a day and dispense with all other meals.

We crossed the Romney Marshes, where sheep in countless thousands crawled like fat, white maggots on a waterlogged emerald blanket. Near Dymchurch, we came upon vestiges of the Invasion That Never Was. Concrete pillboxes were sunk in rank grass, and coils of rusty barbed wire squirmed along the shingle beaches where, in 1941, we had expected the German army to storm ashore. And had wondered how the hell we were going to stop them with our World War I weapons. We would have had a bloody time of it.

In Dover, we stayed at the Hôtel de France which, unfortunately, had been spared destruction by the German seige guns across the Channel on Cap Gris Nez. The food was abominable; the service surly; the bedding damp; and relays of motorcyclists staged impromptu races around the block throughout the night. At dawn the gulls took over, perching on window ledges to scream lewd comments and maledictions at us.

Dover was redeemed by the few hours we spent at an out-of-the-way little pub I had known briefly enough during the winter of 1942 and had cherished for its amiable acceptance of a lonely soldier. I had trouble finding the Four Feathers this time because of the damage done to the neighbourhood by cross-Channel German guns and flying bombs.

The evening was already late when we pushed through the narrow doorway into a snug saloon bar warmed by a coal-burning fireplace and occupied by three middle-aged couples having their quiet pints. We were welcomed with friendly nods and a smile from the balding host behind the bar.

"Been here before, have you?" he asked me as he poured our drinks. "During the fuss, was it?"

"Yes," I said. "Winter of '42. Rotten one too."

"Aye, but we came through all right. With the help of friends from across the water. Friends from Canada, mate. . . . No, the whisky's not for sale to the likes of you tonight. Drink up and have another. The name is Gavin."

We were introduced to the other couples, played darts with them, and chatted together as if we had been companions for a long time. An ex-Commando who had lost an arm at Dieppe insisted we stay over and have dinner with him and his wife next evening. Another couple warmly invited us to come for a week as guests in their cottage on the Isle of Wight. Our glasses were never allowed to stand empty.

When we got back to our gloomy hotel room, Frances seemed somewhat distracted.

"Anything the matter?" I asked.

"Oh, no. It's just that I don't think I've ever spent a nicer evening with nicer people. When Mr. Gavin rang his little bell and flicked the lights and said, 'Time, gentlemen, please,' I almost wanted to cry. . . ."

I knew what she meant.

———————————————

Next morning at the Western Docks we watched fearfully as our pretty little car was seized by a gantry crane, swung high into the sky, then dropped into the ferry's hold. The vessel sailed in such heavy fog that we were not called upon to comment on the white cliffs. The Channel seemed to be alive with shipping — trawlers and little coasters kept materializing close under our stern only to vanish in the mist; we several times had to alter course for big but unseen ships whose presence was made known only by the basso profundo of their horns.

An English version of the Albertan who went from oiling engines to owning oil wells buttonholed us on the foredeck. He described in detail his new Jaguar, his French-built "caravan," his motor yacht, his wife (presumably), and the high esteem in which he was held by his employees. I did not cotton to him and asked what branch of the fighting services he had been with during the war. We did not see him again.

The fog lifted as we came in under Gris Nez. We stared in awe at the monolithic gun emplacements from which the Germans had shelled England. They looked ready to let loose another broadside at any instant, but their day was done. Even before war's end, they had been outmoded by launching ramps from which, in the last year of the war, buzz bombs and V-2 rockets were lobbed at London.

Despite enormous damage and sunken derelicts lying all around the shattered moles, Boulogne harbour functioned well enough. We were offloaded with commendable dispatch.

As usual, I wanted to avoid the main auto routes, so chose back roads that led us up onto the high plateau of the Pas-de-Calais, whose vast fields with their subtle atmosphere of threat were sprinkled with massive plough horses being ridden bare-back and sidesaddle. We did not see a single tractor; even the largest fields were being worked with horses, or by hand. Entire families laboured side by side in the gathering dusk, wielding short-handled hoes over which they bent almost double.

The roads across the plateau ran straight and true between sad rows of stumps — all that remained of tall avenues of plane and poplar trees, hallmarks of the Pas-de-Calais before the war. The ditches were half-filled with piles of richly patinated flints deposited by farmers' barrows. Some had shattered to show their glassy hearts. Here and there, children were at work pick-ing yet more flints from the fields, as their ancestors had been doing since neolithic times.

Small groups of blue-clad road menders straightened their backs as Liz approached, but stared at us with hard, blank faces as we passed. Not all the inhabitants were so reserved. When I stopped to photograph a gnarled oldster on a high-wheeled cart, he leapt sprightly to the tarmac, raced over, and, in an idiom I could barely understand, insisted I send him a copy of the picture when I got back to Chicago.

We tried to find lodging in Beauvais, but all the hotels had been smashed by Allied bombing and the only one that had been restored was fully booked. So we took to the byways again, eventually finding our way to Clermont and a small inn that gave us a bed and a good, if simple, supper.

Clermont people seemed friendly, but someone had painted GO HOME YANKS on the walls of the parking lot, and under it another hand had added A BAS LES ANGLAIS. I was glad that Liz's licence plates displayed the international symbol CDN in large white letters. There are times when it is a comfort to belong to a small nation nobody much hates.

Next morning we encountered Paris. It was a shattering experience. Nobody had briefed us about Parisian drivers. They looked at us, saw we were fearful, and leapt to the attack. They chivvied us, worried us, terrified us. They drove us into cul-de-sacs (that devilish invention of the French) from which we could not easily escape. I had been reduced to a palpitating mound of protoplasm by the time we found the hotel where we had reservations for the night.

It was full. Too bad, *monsieur*, just one of those things — all with a classic Gallic shrug. When I pleaded with the desk clerk, he condescended to give us the name of another inn, the Hôtel Martha, which turned out to be a bleak and dour hole in the wall, filled with bleak, dour people. We got a room on the fifth floor. It was cramped and smelly, and there was no elevator.

Never mind. We were in *Gaie Paris*.

Before we left London, the manager of the Rootes garage

had reminded us to take Liz to the Hillman agency in Paris for a three-hundred-mile check.

"Don't neglect to do so," he had said sternly, "or you may regret it."

Braving ourselves, we set out to find the place, and miraculously succeeded, only to be told that the mechanics were all booked, but we might try again in three or four days. This suggestion was accompanied by another of those damned Gallic shrugs.

I decided to return to the dubious sanctuary of the Martha, but somehow got on Avenue Foch and into the middle of six lanes of traffic. This was too much for Liz. She shuddered and stopped dead. Instantly, we were the focus of a cacophony of fiendish hoots. Drivers thrust heads out of windows and hurled imprecations. A *gendarme* on the sidewalk took one appalled look and fled.

Leaving Frances to hold the fort, I went for help and found an old street cleaner with some of the milk of human kindness left in him. He led me through back streets to a garage where, for a prince's ransom, I prevailed upon a bored mechanic to come and have a look. When he saw the car was a Hillman, he said *merde* a number of times while gesturing passionately towards the vehicles surrounding us. What would you? his gesture said. An *English* car! But, God bless him, he fixed the trouble, which was no more than a loose distributor clamp.

Leaving Liz to calm herself in the hotel parking lot, Fran

and I set out to see the sights on foot. It was not our day. The Eiffel Tower was closed for repairs. We could not find any of the fabled avenues of flowering trees. The air was acrid with exhaust fumes. The dowdiness and joylessness of most of the natives seemed profound. We might as well have been in downtown Toronto or New York. The only people who seemed to be enjoying life were a few American tourists sitting at outdoor café tables, assuring each other that nothing in the world could be more marvellous than to be in Paris Now That Spring Was Here.

Then it began to rain. Not your gentle, Maytime sprinkle either, but a sloshing downpour. We skipped into the nearest restaurant, a rather ornate establishment, seeking shelter, food, and wine. The name of the place — Prunier — had a vaguely familiar ring, but it was not until later that night, when Fran looked it up in our *Guide Michelin*, that we realized we had dined in the haunt of the *crème de la crème* of Parisian gourmets. I can report that the wine was good, the food adequate, the bill colossal.

After a restless night suffering from Napoleon's revenge, we woke determined to remove ourselves from Paris. We packed, paid, and parted from the Hôtel Martha at such an early hour that we were out of the City of Light before the hellish automotive pack realized the prey was gone.

We made a detour to visit Versailles. It was impressive but steeped in melancholy. So much decaying splendour and magnificence; such pretentious squandering of wealth seemed only to epitomize man's growing contempt for, and divorcement from, the natural world, together with his manic compulsion to shape and gild nature for his own pride. The legend inscribed in huge, gold letters along the high eaves of the palace said it all: To the Great Glories of France.

We stopped at a village on Route 6 to buy salami, cheese, bread, and wine. A little farther south, we found a glade on the edge of a woods, where we had a pleasant lunch. I wondered how it was we had this sylvan place all to ourselves. Fran discovered the answer when she went off on an errand of her own. Small signs had been posted on some of the trees, reading simply, Serpents. Although we encountered none of these, we did not linger. I concluded that the person who conceived of that sign as a substitute for Trespassers Will must rank as a genius.

Route 6 was now pulsating with vehicles. Citroëns appeared to be the dominant species. Large Citroëns — big black beasts that took imperious precedence over all others — cut in and out at high speeds with snarling horns. Small Citroëns looked like plumbers' nightmares, but had no evil in them — and not much engine either. There were also hordes of motor scooters, motorcycles, and bicycles with or without tiny gasoline motors attached. All were taking advantage of a Friday holiday to flee Paris, a decision Fran and I could heartily applaud.

By the time we reached Auxerre in the valley of the Yonne, the face of France had begun to relax. Warmth and colour were becoming evident. This was not yet the south but neither did it display the austere, often baleful countenance of the north.

Because we liked the name, we chose to spend the night at Le Chapeau Rouge in Avallon. The hotel was welcoming and comfortable, and the town, perched on a granite rock overlooking a placid river, was a delight. Leaving Liz to chew her cud, we walked down steep and crowded streets to find that Avallon was having a party in honour of the *maquis* — the wartime Resistance fighters.

After a five-course dinner in a small café that rivalled, if it did not surpass, Monsieur Prunier's, we meandered into the heart of the old town, picking our way between gaily striped refreshment tents, enjoying the crowds of colourfully dressed and laughing people, and pausing at outdoor cafés to refresh ourselves.

During one such halt a man wearing a *maquis* beret gave us good evening, and forthrightly asked who we were and what we were doing in Avallon.

When I explained that I was a veteran of the Canadian army and we were retracing my wartime footsteps, he bowed low to Fran, kissed me fervently, and slapped his beret on my head.

"But how wonderful! We are comrades! You and your beautiful wife must help celebrate our victory over *les Boches*!"

Bertrand brooked no arguments. Taking us one on either arm, he guided us into the crowd, stopping here and there to enthusiastically introduce us to his many friends. It was as if we had been born in Avallon and had returned after a long absence. Nothing was too good for us. We visited so many cafés and drank so many toasts in so many varied wines that Fran and I lost count of everything, including time. I remember marching behind brass bands in the blue-clad ranks of Resistance fighters, being dazzled by fireworks, and, vaguely, being escorted back to our hotel by a crowd singing *Auprès de ma blonde* at the top of their voices. Apparently I had told someone it was my favourite song.

We departed Avallon with reluctance, latish on Saturday morning, being under the necessity of reaching Lyon in time to have Liz serviced before Sunday closed that city down.

Route 6 now took us down the lush valley of the Saône. We ate a good omelette at a roadside café whose sweating, whitewashed walls were as refreshing to the eye on this hot day as the cool local wine was to the palate.

Approaching Mâcon, we saw a flock of flying saucers glittering over a row of trees. I attributed this vision to the wine but when, a few minutes later, we opened onto a broad plain, the saucers resolved themselves into French army parachutists practising their trade. They needed practice. I prevented one of them from landing in the car (our top was down) only by taking skilful evasive action.

Some hours later we mounted the shoulder of a great hill to find Lyon sprawled smokily below us. It was late in the day, but we tracked down the Hillman agency, where I shamelessly bribed a mechanic to service the car by early next morning.

We dined at a nearby brasserie on snails, *bifteck* that had a distinctly equine flavour, and Bordeaux. Towards the end of the meal, Fran evidenced symptoms of food poisoning and fainted. A posse of waiters revived her with some unknown cordial and I carried her back to our charmless, modern hotel. We were beginning to wonder if all the cities we visited were conspiring to lay a curse upon us.

But no. The Lyon garage mechanic turned out to be as good as his word (and as my francs). He telephoned at 9:00 A.M. to tell us Liz was ready for the fray.

There being no further need to stick to the principal routes, we headed eastward along a single-lane road towards the foothills of the French Alps. This was good country, displaying an easygoing luxuriance not to be found in the penurious north. Instead of unlovely huddles of grey stone buildings engulfed by vast bare fields, farms here were rambling concoctions of mellowed yellow brick roofed with burnt-red tiles, sprawling at ease amongst vineyards, meadows, and graceful orchards.

We climbed into this pleasant land over a succession of ridges, each steeper and higher than the last. We chose the crest of one for our luncheon halt and munched bread and cheese and drank wine while watching a flock of sportive crows soaring far below. Then a long switchback descent took us into the valley of the Isère, where we diverted along a dirt track to the tiny village of Chatte.

Chatte was home to a young French anthropologist who had recently visited the Inuit I had written about in *People of the Deer*. We had arranged to meet here but he had unexpectedly been called to Paris. Nevertheless, we were made welcome to a whitewashed cottage by his mother and grandmother. In the cool depths of dark, old rooms, they gave us cakes and wine and would have had us stay the night, but Fran had not recovered from her *malaise lyonnais* and I thought it wiser to get her to a hotel where she could rest.

Vercors

In Lyon I had studied our maps and *Michelin*, looking for a suitable place to hole up for a few days. A village called Villard-de-Lans, tucked away in the mountains not far beyond Chatte, had caught my eye. It was well off the beaten track and, according to *Michelin*, was notable for its fresh air, natural surroundings, and wholesome hotels.

An almost sheer mountain wall faced us on the far side of the Isère. We crossed the river gorge towards it on an ancient suspension bridge, swaying uneasily a hundred feet above the bottom of the canyon. The hamlet of Pont-en-Royans crouched under soaring crags on the east bank. As we eased through its one narrow street, villagers made cautionary gestures, pointing to the cliffs above, and one of them called out, "*Mon*

Dieu, monsieur, that little English car will not survive!"

I passed this off as good-natured chaff.

Just beyond the village, the single-lane road turned abruptly towards the crags to enter a narrow cleft from which rushed a mountain stream. At first, road and stream ran side by side at the bottom of a V-shaped slit a thousand feet deep. Soon, however, the track (it was a road only by courtesy) began angling up the steep northern wall.

There were no guard rails. Rough-hewn tunnels not much wider than the car burrowed through overhangs. As we climbed, the gorge climbed with us so that we seemed to be getting no nearer the top, but a hell of a long way from the bottom. The stream diminished in our view until it was no more than a gossamer thread.

As if this ascent was not fearsome enough, I was having to contend with a plague of Citroëns and Renaults descending at full speed from unknown heights, horns blasting as they demanded the right of way. I turned on Liz's lights and rested my wrist on her horn button. Time after time I had to squeeze into passing spaces to avoid the suicidal charges of these demented projectiles. They whizzed by us in blind tunnels, and at right-angle bends where I swear our wheels kicked gravel into the deepening abyss.

I would have retreated, but there was no place to turn around. So we crawled on, climbing in low gear and sweating it out as we awaited the next Citroën assault. Eventually the track branched away from the main gorge up a smaller ravine and, after worming its way over a long, barren col, emerged into the vale of Vercors.

Before us lay a high plateau ringed by snow-capped peaks. Pine forests darkened the lower slopes, but the undulating valley floor was awash in the vibrant verdancy of alpine pastures. Clusters of red-tiled farm buildings were scattered along wooded streams, or on highland fields dusted with grazing sheep and cattle. The town of Villard-de-Lans drowsed in brilliant sunshine in the middle of the plateau.

The mountain track we had been following became a well-mannered road again, winding its way sedately towards the little town through plantations of young spruce and pine. My white-knuckled grip on Liz's steering wheel slowly relaxed.

We stopped in the immaculately tidy central square to inquire about hotels. A boy on a bicycle directed us up a steep little street to a vast, barn-like chalet called Hôtel de Paris. The name rather put us off until a white-haired old man, wearing a blue beret and a peasant's smock, came out to greet us. Doffing his beret, he made a sweeping bow, and welcomed us . . . to heaven, or at least to haven.

The staff, who all appeared to be female except for the old porter, received us with an excess of zeal, flashing about the wide, white halls with armfuls of feather quilts, hot-water bottles, a flagon of cognac, and other things thought needful to our comfort. Shortly we found ourselves in possession of a big, airy room, whose several large windows looked east and north to white-capped mountains.

A fine figure of a negress named Marie made us her special charge, insisting on carrying our luggage to the room, then interrogating us in a delightful Creole accent as to the state of our health. When she discovered Fran was not at her best, Marie turned on me like a black panther.

"What a way you treat this *petite pauvre, monsieur*. To take her up *les gorges de la Bourne* on a *Sunday*! It is to have no heart!"

"Why is that?" I asked meekly, for she overtopped me by half a head.

Having first poured a drink of cognac into Fran and settled her in the high bed for a rest, Marie condescended to explain.

I learned there are only three routes into the Vercors, and only two fit for automobiles. The one we had ascended was considered the most scenic drive in France, but also the most dangerous. Every Sunday young bloods from the city of Grenoble, on Vercors's northern boundary, drove up to Villard-de-Lans through the relatively easy Gorges d'Engins, then descended at top speed down the gorges of the Bourne, treating it as a roller-coaster-cum-hell driver's challenge. Nobody in his right mind, Marie told us, would attempt an *ascent* of the Bourne on a Sunday. Unless, she added, one was tired of life and seeking a spectacular departure from it.

Leaving Fran in Marie's capable hands, I set out to explore the town. The stone houses of its five hundred residents were low and broad and jammed together as if to better resist winter storms. Although lacking the colourful eccentricities of Swiss alpine architecture, they looked comfortable; and so did the people I met along the way, most of whom had a smile or a nod for a stranger.

The Café du Sport tempted me. I found it full of smartly dressed young men and women from Grenoble tanking up preparatory to dicing with death in the Bourne gorges. The waiter who brought me my Pernod was a mine of gruesome information about this local form of entertainment.

"Me, I would not go down that road without a parachute. Last week a Peugeot missed a turn and flew so far out over the valley it landed a kilometre to the east and five hundred metres below the road. It blew up like a bomb and burned. A friend of mine saw it go. He said the flames seemed no bigger than a match, it had flown so far away."

He made me nervous. I drained my glass and hurried back to the hotel.

There was only a handful of other guests in the great dining room, but the meal was superb. It began with a truffle-flavoured soup, followed by *truite meunière* (the trout having been caught that very afternoon in a mountain stream), veal *aux fines herbes*, hearts of artichoke salad, *chocolat glacé*, and an array of cheeses.

We were served by Marie, who was clearly a woman of many parts. When (perhaps still a little shaken by our experiences in the gorges) I sprinkled icing sugar from a silver shaker into my soup instead of salt, she instantly spotted the gaffe and, sweeping down like a hawk, snatched the bowl away. Replacing it with a fresh one, she gave me a lecture, illustrated with gestures, on the identification and use of condiment containers. I was grateful there were so few other diners.

She made amends next morning by bringing us breakfast in bed, unasked. As Fran and I luxuriated over frothy scrambled eggs and crumbly croissants, Marie entertained us with an account of her carefree childhood in Martinique, followed by a truncated but nevertheless Rabelaisian description of her life in a superior bordello in Marseille. After contracting tuberculosis there, she retreated to a sanatorium in the Vercors. Cured, she decided to stay on and, in due course, became the indispensable mainstay of the Hôtel de Paris. Had she ever married? Fran wanted to know. Marie grinned.

"*Mais non!* Never will I marry! Not so long as there are poor, sad men without love in the world."

Not only was she a singularly effective woman, she was a dedicated one as well.

Beyond our broad windows, the mountains called. Next morning we drove up the valley to a newly built *téléférique* — ski lift — expecting to climb the mountains the easy way. But the machine was closed so we set out on foot, working our way upward until we reached an open pine forest where spring had but newly arrived. A snow-cooled breeze tempered the sun's heat and I was filled with an urge to scale a peak. Frances sensibly decided to relax on the warm moss.

I climbed for a mile through thinning woods, crossed an alpine meadow where edelweiss glowed its unearthly blue, and came to the edge of a thawing snow field. As I rested on a rock pinnacle, I had the whole plateau at my feet.

The Vercors massif stands apart from the main bulk of the Alps like a titanic island. It is roughly triangular, some thirty-five miles from north to south, and twenty from east to west. The high ranges that wall it in plunge five thousand feet to the three bordering river valleys of the Isère, the Drac, and the Drôme, which, together, form a moat around what is, in effect, a gargantuan natural bastion. Gazing out across its wooded ridges and verdant valleys, I indulged myself in a Shangri-La fantasy about a mountain domain forever isolated from the contamination of the outside world.

Sniffing the richness of new growth, I slowly descended through the seasons from late winter to early summer to rejoin a sleepy Frances, who had been dozing in the sun. Then, still in an exploring mood, we drove south along the foot of the mountains along a rutted cart track.

We had gone only a mile or so when our progress was literally reduced to an oxen's pace. We had caught up to a train of five teams of long-horned, cream-coloured beasts, each team skidding a bundle of two or three logs down the centre of the track.

These were not logs in the North American sense of the word. They were entire trees, shorn only of their branches. Each was about a foot and a half in diameter at the butt, tapering for some fifty feet to a diameter of two or three inches. They looked like giant toothpicks.

A young man with the build of Charles Atlas was driving the last team. He fell back to saunter beside the car and make conversation. He told us his name was Gérard, one of five brothers who owned and worked a small sawmill near the hamlet of Corrençon, which lay just ahead.

"You are from Canada, the land of the loomber-Jacques, is it not? So you must come to the mill and meet my brothers. There may be much you can tell us to make better the way we work."

It turned out to be the other way around. *I* was the one who learned from the Molyneaux brothers how skilled, conscientious, and long-sighted foresters and sawyers manage their woodland resources. It was something of a revelation.

All the feeder valleys running up into the high slopes were thickly wooded, despite the fact that they had been lumbered for countless centuries. Gérard told me that, for every tree cut down, three seedlings had to be planted. The management plan required not only that existing forests be maintained, but that they be improved and, where possible, enlarged. If a landowner failed to meet these requirements his timber licence was withdrawn. The intention was that, even if the Vercors continued to be inhabited for another thousand years, it would remain well forested.

The rule of the regional forester was absolute. He and his staff ensured only mature trees were cut, and selectively, in a here-and-there pattern that did not injure the forest as an entity.

Each tree to be felled was chosen by a professional forester. The owner's crew then took the tree down at ground level, so there would be no stump wastage. The bole was trimmed of branches, but not "topped" except for the growing tip; the debris was broken up and spread out over the forest floor to rot. Finally, the trimmed bole was carefully "snaked" out of the woods by horses or oxen so as to avoid damage to new growth.

When the ox train (trailed by Liz, looking distinctly incongruous) reached the mill, the logs were rolled off the road, and we were invited into an open-sided sawing shed, there to be introduced to three more of the brothers. Georges, the mill boss, was a long-faced man with black eyes and a lopsided grin, who was happy to show us around.

The mill was surprisingly quiet, so much so that the splash of rushing water from the race that powered the machinery could be clearly heard. The ear-splitting scream of mighty circular saws was absent. In their place was an array of thin-bladed band saws.

"These waste but little wood," Georges explained. "In Canada, you can perhaps afford to make much sawdust with your circular saws. We cannot. See?" He pointed to the outside yard. "No sawdust pile."

A sawmill without an adjacent sawdust mountain seemed an anomaly to me. Another significant difference was the absence of a slab pile. I watched a log enter the mill. No slabs were trimmed from it to be subsequently discarded. Not even the bark was removed. The entire log was band-sawed into planks that were then piled in sequence, separated only by little spacers to allow the wood to dry. If there was to be any wastage, carpenters, not sawyers, would be responsible.

Georges told me that local carpenters and woodworkers *preferred* the whole plank. "It is because they can choose the shape and size of the piece they want exactly, and so waste little."

When the Molyneaux brothers questioned me about lumbering in Canada, I had no improvements to offer, but I did tentatively suggest that the practices they followed might not be as profitable as ours.

"Waste," I said, "*makes* profits in our country. Fifteen to twenty percent of all the wood we cut and mill is lost in the process. But waste enables our people to mass-produce their products and so sell more of them. You see?"

Georges and his brothers looked puzzled. I was afraid they might want me to elucidate, and I wasn't sure I wanted to.

Gérard sighed. "*Eh, bien*. People do things differently in different places. Perhaps now you and your *belle femme* would like a glass of wine?"

The wine was raw but strong, and we talked no more of waste and profits. Instead, I spoke admiringly of the local oxen — and discovered they were not. Laughing, Gérard pointed out that the big tawny beasts were all cows — milch cows at that. They might work for part of the day, lumbering or ploughing, then they went to pasture and at night yielded up their milk. Vercors was full of surprises.

———————————————

After a few days of easy walks, prodigious meals, and sleeping long and late, Fran was recovering her stamina, but was not yet inclined for demanding adventures. One morning I set out on my own to really climb a mountain. I chose the Col de l'Arc, which, at seven thousand feet, was not the highest peak in the massif, but high enough.

It turned out that I had bitten off far more than I could climb. Discretion, and spots before my eyes, halted me before a vertical rock face five thousand feet up. After recovering my wind, I angled off to one side and came upon a goat track worn into the flank of the crag. Rock slides had carried sections of it away, but I was able to follow it and I could look out over the Vercors from such an altitude it felt like being in a helicopter, without the noise and nuisance.

A ceiling of opalescent cloud hung just above my head while the sun shone brilliantly below. A pair of falcons shot swiftly past, and cliff-nesting ravens swirled about, calling raucously. I came to a man-sized niche in the rock and, nestled on wet moss within it, found several greening rifle cartridges bearing French army markings. Their presence puzzled me. In this high isolation there would have been no game to shoot; but, looking down, I saw three tiny human figures walking on a distant road.

The cloud began to lower and I felt a chill of unease. Time to go. I pocketed one of the empty casings and hurried to retrace my way.

I found the old porter (who seemed to be known only as Monsieur Pierre) sitting on a bench by the door of the hotel, pulling at his pipe. I joined him and we smoked in companionable silence for a while. Then I took the cartridge case from my pocket, showed it to him, and asked if there had been fighting in the Vercors.

He looked at me in astonishment.

"Is it possible, *monsieur*, you do not know?"

I shook my head and asked, "Tell me what happened?"

He seemed reluctant to oblige. Instead, he suggested I drive to a place called the Belvédère.

"It will speak to you, that place," he said.

After dinner, Fran and I went in search of the Belvédère. As we drove along a winding gravel track through sombre pine plantations, slowly climbing into a sky-high valley, we began passing small roadside monuments. I stopped to look at one. It bore a plaque engraved with the words, *Souvenir de*, followed by the names of ten men and women, and concluding with *mort pour la France*.

We passed a dozen of these little shrines, but none offered any explanation as to when or how the people memorialized on them had died.

At length we came around a curve on the high flank of a wooded mountain. Here, in the shadow of an overhanging crag, an abutment had been built out over the valley. On the lip of this ledge, almost suspended in space, stood a tall, slim cross. This was the Belvédère.

It commanded a mighty vista. An arm of the Bourne gorges, dwarfed to wormish insignificance, crawled into the mountains an infinite distance below us. Minuscule fields clung to rocky slopes, and we could see scattered farm buildings that appeared to be in ruins. A quarter of a mile up the valley to the south, an orchard blossomed in random glory around a small village.

No smoke rose from its houses. No living being moved in the gathering dusk.

Leaving Liz, we followed a narrow track down to that village, and ours were the only human footsteps to mar a carpet of waxen white flowers stretching before us all the way.

We found a dozen stone houses clustered in a setting so magnificent as to make their shattered state seem especially hideous. Each was no more than a crumbling shell from which young trees were sprouting, drawing strength from the decay of fire-blackened beams and rafters. The gaping doorway of a ruined *bureau de poste* was flanked by a blackened letter box whose metal door swung gently in the evening breeze. It was the only thing that moved in the village of Valchevrière.

The illusion of bucolic peace that had seemed to invest Vercors was abruptly dissipated.

Whatever had taken place on the plateau in the not-so-distant past had evidently been so horrendous that the inhabitants did not wish to talk about it or, at any rate, not to strangers. We might never have been much the wiser had not Monsieur Pierre intimated that one of the few other guests of the hotel, a nondescript and pallid middle-aged man with a pronounced limp, might be willing to enlighten us.

"M. Tenant was himself in Vercors during those times. He was of the staff of Commandant Hervioux, *chef de la Résistance* here. He comes now for his health, which is not good. Perhaps if you tell him you, too, were a soldier who fought against *les allemandes* . . ."

Next day I encountered Pierre Tenant in the hotel grounds and introduced myself. At first he was merely polite but, after I had casually referred to my military experience in Italy, he warmed. We walked together to the Café du Sport for an aperitif. As we returned to the hotel, he volunteered: "Vercors people do not wish to be reminded of those terrible times, you understand. They were so terrible I would not blame them if they hated us who were of the *Résistance* for, in a way, it was we who brought so much horror upon them. It was a tragedy for all." He paused. "Well, perhaps, monsieur, *I* can tell you something of what happened."*

Pierre Tenant wrote a book about his experiences with the Secret Army in Vercors. It is called Vercors — Haute-Lieu de France.

Fall of a Fortress

IN the aftermath of the collapse of the French Republic in 1940, Mussolini's troops invaded the southern provinces and occupied Grenoble.

The Italians tended to be easygoing, content to exercise nominal control over major cities while allowing life in the countryside to proceed as usual. Because of this and because of the moral vacuum in France, their presence roused little active resistance. Most Frenchmen sullenly accepted defeat, but a few were not so compliant and as early as 1941 had begun organizing for the day when the armies of France might live again.

In the spring of 1942 the collaborationist Vichy government sanctioned the conscription of young Frenchmen for forced labour in Germany. This sent numbers of young men fleeing into the Vercors massif to conceal themselves in farms and lumber camps in the high forests and alpine valleys. They were not yet *maquis* — guerrillas. At this juncture they wished only to hide.

Down in the city of Grenoble, older men noted the drift of youngsters into Vercors and began nurturing dreams. Officers of the regular army, now calling itself the Secret Army, conceived a bold and romantic plan. Considering Vercors's unique nature, these officers envisaged the massif transformed into an actual fortress, an island of freedom in the heart of Nazi Europe manned by soldiers of Free France.

During the winter of 1942-43 the plans were implemented. Soldiers from many places in France heard the clandestine call to arms and made their way secretly to Vercors.

The Italians seem to have been unaware of what was happening; at any rate, they took no effective action to prevent it. Within months the massif belonged to the Secret Army. The gates of the fortress closed so quietly the Italians did not hear them shut.

By the spring of 1943 the dream had become a reality. Vercors *was* an islet of freedom in an enslaved continent. The Secret Army had established a network of training camps and, by mid-year, was ready to go to war.

There were enough soldiers, but few weapons except sporting rifles, shotguns, and pistols. This lack was remedied in part by raids on Italian convoys on the roads outside Vercors. Enough military rifles and machine guns were acquired to support a bolder stroke, and in July the Vercors army staged a successful raid on the city of Grenoble itself, headquarters of the Italian occupation force, and succeeded in carrying off several truckloads of guns and ammunition.

The Secret Army consisted of two groups. First was a professional force under Capitaine Léon Goderville, a regular army officer. Then there was the civilian *maquis* under the command of René Clermont, a lawyer from Villard-de-Lans. A joint combat committee co-ordinated the two forces and oversaw auxiliary services.

The Vercors army waged an effective guerrilla war against the occupying Italians until late in 1943, when Italy capitulated to the Allies. The Italian garrisons in France were immediately replaced by Germans, and thereafter the Secret Army faced a much more formidable foe. Nevertheless, it continued to carry the battle to the enemy. A mixed force of 325 regular soldiers and 300 members of the *maquis* began harassing the new German occupation troops in the surrounding region.

The Germans were soon smarting from the attacks and, unlike the Italians, could be counted on to strike back. Goderville and Clermont knew it would only be a matter of time before the fortress would have to repel an assault. But during the hard winter of 1943 a shortage of food and weapons forced the commanders to temporarily disband half their army and send the men to shelter with the civilian populace outside the walls of the massif.

At this critical juncture René Clermont undertook to make his way out of France in a bid to obtain significant material aid from the Allies.

After a month-long clandestine journey of epic proportions, including a voyage across the Mediterranean in a motor torpedo boat stolen from the Vichy navy, he reached Algiers. There, staff officers of the Allied command in North Africa listened attentively as Clermont assured them that, given the weapons, the Army of Vercors could hold the fortress indefinitely. He also stressed the enormous possibilities Vercors offered as a break-out point from which to strike at the rear of the German lines when the Second Front opened. We can even build an airfield for you, Clermont told the generals.

The Allied planners were impressed. Landed back in southern France by a British submarine, Clermont returned to Vercors through the Resistance underground, bearing the promise of immediate and substantial Allied help.

It could come none too soon. In late December, during Clermont's absence, the three hundred effectives remaining in Vercors had staged a brilliantly successful raid on the German garrison in Grenoble, killing a number of enemy soldiers and destroying much material.

Stung to fury, the Germans struck back. On January 22 Lieutenant Chabal, commanding a platoon of *maquis*, was driving a truckload of his men down the Bourne gorges to relieve an outpost when he spotted the head of a German armoured column on the twisting road far below. Chabal ordered his men to jump clear, but himself drove on at full speed towards the enemy. At the last moment he leaped from the cab and rolled into a ditch, while his truck smashed headlong into a German armoured half-track. The ensuing mêlée took the invaders an hour to clear — sufficient time for news of the attack to be flashed across the fortress.

Goderville had prayed no major German attack would occur until spring, by which time — if Clermont's mission succeeded — there might be enough weapons to properly arm the garrison. As things stood, the three hundred badly armed men who were all he now had available could not hope to withstand a full-scale assault.

When he heard that a second German armoured column had overrun the defences of Saint-Nizier — Vercors's northern gate — Goderville knew what he had to do. Rather than attempt a suicidal defence, he made "the bitterest decision of my life" by ordering his forces to break contact and withdraw. Within hours they had faded away into the mountains and the high forests.

It was not a rout. The Secret Army had staged a carefully prepared vanishing act designed to leave nothing behind that would betray the army's true size, organization, and potential.

In this the defenders were successful. Although the Germans

overran the valleys of Vercors, they were deluded as to the strength of the opposition, supposing it to consist of no more than a handful of *maquis* who had now been effectively and permanently dispersed. However, to ensure that guerrillas would give no more trouble, savage reprisals were taken.

Six Secret Army men wounded and captured at Saint-Nizier were shot out of hand. Six local farmers accused of harbouring terrorists were executed, in front of their families. Saint-Nizier was razed and many farmhouses in the gorges of the Bourne were dynamited. As many young men as could be found were rounded up and shipped to Buchenwald. Satisfied then that all potential for resistance had been eliminated, the German military withdrew.

They quitted Vercors in mid-April. By mid-May the whole of the fortress was once again in French hands — and this time the gates were iron-barred.

Soon after Clermont's return, Allied air drops had begun. Spring brought an end to the food shortage. Goderville sent his messengers into the countryside, and the balance of the army returned to the fortress where there were now weapons enough to arm every man.

On June 6 news of the invasion of Normandy was received, together with an order from Free French headquarters instructing all units of the French Interior Forces (as the Resistance was now officially known), to take the offensive. U.S. Flying Fortresses and British Lancasters began droning over the Vercors mountains by day and by night to drop supplies. A British mission was parachuted in, together with a section of American Rangers. DeGaulle's Free French sent engineer specialists to supervise construction of an airstrip upon which substantial Allied forces could be landed. During one two-day period filled with the roar of aero-engines, Allied bombers dropped six hundred containers of small arms and ammunition around the village of Vassieux, where the landing field was being built.

On June 9 Goderville was succeeded by Commandant Hervioux. The forces then available to the new commander included five companies of *maquis* totalling fifteen hundred men and four battalions of regular army troops totalling nearly three thousand. It was time to go on the offensive.

Units from Vercors struck at German supply routes over a broad area of southeastern France. They did so much damage and posed such a threat that the enemy had to divert some twenty thousand men from the vital battle for Normandy in an attempt to deal with them. On June 13, barely six weeks after they had left Vercors believing they had "pacified" it, the Germans were forced to attempt to recapture it.

General Erik Pflaum, commanding the campaign, resolved to make it a quick one. At dawn on June 13 he attacked from Saint-Nizier with a complete infantry brigade supported by tanks and a regiment of artillery.

Four hundred Secret Army men armed mainly with rifles, machine guns, grenades, and machine pistols barred the way.

They stopped the German attack in the Gorges d'Engins and not only threw the enemy back but captured three 75mm mountain howitzers, which they turned on the German transport below with devastating effect.

The Germans replied with salvo after salvo of heavy artillery fire, but the French would not be budged.

Late in the afternoon Commandant Hervioux radioed an urgent appeal to Algiers for more ammunition. That night some two hundred containers were dropped by RAF Lancasters.

The Germans renewed the battle at dawn. Mortar and shellfire on the rocky slopes of the gorge became so heavy that the defenders began a phased withdrawal, forcing the Germans to advance through deadly flanking fire. On the afternoon of June 14, ammunition again began to run low. Again Hervioux radioed Algiers, but that night no bombers were available.

The defenders fell back to positions high up on the slopes from which they could enfilade the Germans emerging onto the open valley floor.

The enemy advance guard managed to push only a mile or two into the Lans Valley before coming under such sustained small-arms fire from the mountains that General Pflaum was forced to order a general withdrawal.

During their retreat down the Gorges d'Engins, the Germans exacted savage vengeance. Thirteen captured Secret Army men were murdered and mutilated, their corpses left strewn along the twisting road as object lessons. Every remaining structure on the invasion route was dynamited or burned. Captured civilians were herded out of the massif, thrown into internment camps, and later shipped to slave labour camps in Germany.

Nevertheless, the victory raised the morale of the defenders to new heights and brought an influx of volunteers from the surrounding regions. Vercors now became the rallying point for the Resistance in areas as far distant as Lyon. Couriers arrived nightly, bringing information or asking for arms.

One night a young woman with a shock of black hair falling over her eyes was brought to Hervioux's command post. When asked her business, she claimed to be the leader of a *maquis* band near Valence in urgent need of guns.

"We were suspicious, naturally. She might have been a Gestapo agent," Tenant remembered. "It was my task to question her. We gave her a difficult time, but in the end were satisfied that Marie-Jean — her code name — was indeed leader of a band of men carrying out effective raids on German transport."

Marie got her guns. A week later she and her group ambushed a convoy of German trucks. The Germans counterattacked in force, killing all of Marie's men and wounding and capturing her. Temporarily imprisoned in the upstairs room of a farmhouse, she jumped from a window and escaped. She then travelled for three nights, hiding by day, before reaching the home of a friend where she lay for several weeks until her wounds healed. Meanwhile, the Germans had discovered her real identity and arrested her father. When the old man failed to give any useful information, he was shot. Marie survived to rejoin the *maquis*, take an active part in the liberation of Lyon, and be decorated with the Cross of Honour.

There were less violent incidents. The garrison of Vichy gendarmes stationed in the village of Saint-Marcellin on the Isère River decided to join the Vercors army. However, they were local men and knew their families would be subjected to severe reprisals if they deserted. One of them thought of a way to deal with the problem. A message was sent to the *maquis* suggesting that an attack be made on Saint-Marcellin on a given night. Although the garrison would put up a spirited defence, they would be firing into the air. The attackers were expected to be equally thoughtful.

On the appointed night frightened townsfolk cowered in their cellars as gunfire rippled through the streets. The gendarmes fought so valiantly before being "captured" that their bereaved families were given extra rations by the grateful Vichy authorities.

The no-longer-secret army was now very busy. Raid after raid was launched on German outposts and supply columns. On July 10 a force supported by the U.S. Ranger section ambushed a convoy of more than fifty German vehicles and destroyed most of them without losing a man. These operations were so successful that the countryside for miles around was effectively freed from German control. Main highways running near Vercors were denied to the enemy, and German garrisons had to be evacuated from the towns of Die, Romans, and several others.

Hervieux was an imaginative commander. One day he sent a detachment of his men into Grenoble itself to fetch some three thousand French Army uniforms secretly cached there in 1940. When their trucks were halted by German control posts, the raiders produced forged Vichy papers showing they were under orders to move a load of "waste clothing" south to a refugee camp. They were allowed to pass, and soon thereafter a good part of the ragged army of Vercors was transformed into properly uniformed soldiers of the French army.

The Germans in Grenoble were now themselves virtually under seige; the railroads were unusable, and their vital highway links closed except when they could dispatch tanks and armoured cars to guard the convoys. Because of the near certainty of an Allied invasion of southern France, it was strategically necessary that Grenoble be held, but, despite the fact that two divisions had now been diverted from Normandy where every available German soldier was desperately needed, Grenoble remained at risk.

The situation worsened for the Germans on June 14 when a massed daylight flight of two hundred Flying Fortresses dropped a thousand containers of arms and ammunition around

Vassieux. It did not require much imagination on the part of the German staff to comprehend the consequences had those parachutes been weighted with Allied paratroops. There was still more bad news. German air reconnaissance revealed the landing field under construction near Vassieux.

It was apparent to the *Wehrmacht* General Staff that drastic action had to be taken, else Grenoble, the key to the defences of the southern Alps, would be lost.

The decision was made. Three squadrons of ME 109 fighters were detached from the crucial struggle in Normandy and flown to airports near Vercors. Infantry, artillery, and tank units urgently needed elsewhere were diverted to Grenoble. General Pflaum received orders of the highest priority to take the fortress.

Resistance agents kept Hervioux informed of what was brewing. Although the moment of decision was at hand, he was not unduly worried. By July 25 his airfield would be ready to receive the first Dakota transport planes. Once a modicum of artillery, mortars, and anti-tank guns had reached him, nothing the Germans could do would seriously threaten the fortress.

By July 15 the tension had become acute. Work on the airfield was ahead of schedule, but meantime the vital need for support weapons was not being met. Hervioux repeatedly radioed Algiers, asking for mountain guns and mortars to be dropped by parachute or even sent in by glider. Everything hung on what could be done in the next ten days. Day after day his pleas remained unanswered.

The *Luftwaffe* seized daylight command of the air space over the massif. Lacking anti-aircraft defence, the inhabitants were forced to take cover during daylight hours. Construction of the airfield could continue only at night. Nevertheless, work went forward until only three days remained before the first transports would be able to land, bringing the vital heavy weapons upon which Vercors's fate depended.

On the afternoon of July 20, a telephone in Hervioux's headquarters rang sharply.

An observation post on a crag overlooking Grenoble reported a continuous stream of German troops, tanks, armoured vehicles, and artillery pieces moving out of the city.

Other posts began reporting in. German assault columns were driving south under both the eastern and western flanks of the massif. By noon advance elements had reached Clermont on the west and Saint-Marcellin on the east. A huge enveloping movement, intended to enclose the whole of the massif within an iron ring, was being executed. When the ring was closed the attack on the fortress would begin.

Bent over battle maps at his command post, Hervioux watched the circle close. Turning to his staff, he said quietly, "Gentlemen, the great adventure has begun."

At 6:00 A.M. on July 21, more than twenty-five thousand German troops, including five artillery regiments, many tanks, and three squadrons of fighter-bombers, attacked the fortress.

Three battalions of infantry supported by tanks and mobile guns thrust towards the Lans plain from the ruins of Saint-Nizier. By 8:00 A.M. they were within rifle range of a platoon commanded by Second Lieutenant Bertrand Noel, a twenty-year-old Free French officer who had been parachuted into Vercors. Although his was supposed to be only a skirmishing role, Noel chose to stand and fight. A hail of small-arms fire forced the enemy column to deploy. In the face of ferocious tank and artillery shelling, Noel and his men held their ground. Only after seven defenders had been killed and another ten wounded did the survivors slip away.

The Germans paused briefly to lick their wounds. When the advance began again it did so in two columns, and much more cautiously. One headed north across the Lans plain in an attempt to seize the commanding heights, where I found the greening cartridge cases many years later. It was met by Capitaine Albert Duffans and three hundred members of the *maquis* who, from their mountain eyries, kept that column pinned down and unable to advance during the following two days and nights.

Meanwhile, the second and larger column continued cautiously up the Lans Valley. Hervioux planned to allow it to advance almost to Villard-de-Lans and into a prepared killing ground where it would then come under fire from four hundred of the best troops in Vercors. If this ambush succeeded, the German assault could be turned into a débâcle.

It was now mid-morning. Service troops were standing by at the almost-completed landing field to receive a long-awaited air drop. The roar of many engines was heard and cheering men emerged from cover, running towards the drop zone. The aircraft came over the surrounding mountain rim out of the morning sun, thundering a message of hope.

The lead echelon wheeled, dived steeply and, as a blast of machine-gun and cannon fire raked the airstrip, those on the ground saw black swastikas on the wings above them.

Time after time, flights of ME 109 fighter-bombers and JU 87 dive-bombers strafed the open fields and everything that moved on them. . . . And then . . . fifty JU 88 transports came lumbering over the valley disgorging a rain of parachutists.

Even before the paratroops had reached the ground, a second fleet of transports was overhead, cutting loose gliders laden with artillery and heavy mortars. Here, at last, were the heavy weapons the defenders of Vercors had so urgently requested — but they belonged to the grey-clad soldiers of the Reich.

The airfield was soon a shambles. Captain Hardy, commanding the British Liaison mission, and most of his men were dead. Lieutenant Paquebot, a French officer in charge of building the strip, was fatally wounded. One of his crew, Victor Vermorel, ran to the only machine gun on the field and sprayed the descending enemy until he was hit in the chest. Captured shortly afterwards, he died from a pistol bullet in the back of his skull. The paratroopers were SS men, who took no prisoners. All civilians found in the nearby houses, to the number of sixty-seven men, women, and children, were butchered. Wounded men of the reception group were massacred with hand grenades.

When the terrible news reached Hervioux, he knew that victory had escaped him. He had no option but to withdraw the four hundred from the ambush position at Villard-de-Lans and commit them against the parachutists at Vassieux. Hurrying to the scene of the air landing, these troops managed to establish a ring about the airfield, which was now in the hands of an entire SS paratroop brigade. The forging and holding of that ring by the four hundred was an epic in war's annals.

There was bravery in plenty, but bravery was not enough. Although the major ground assault had been directed into the Lans plain, another German column was attacking up the Gorges of the Bourne while a division of German mountain troops assaulted the passes in the southwest. The weight of the attack grew heavier by the hour.

In front of Villard-de-Lans a *single platoon* under Capitaine Brissac now took on the task originally allocated to four hundred men. Brissac held firm until his platoon was annihilated and he himself dead. Then the Germans pressed on to occupy Corrençon and close their grip on the whole of the Lans Valley.

Elsewhere the news was somewhat better. The French

were successful in holding all the passes in the southwest, and the encirclement of the SS brigade at the airport remained unbroken despite the arrival by glider of another SS paratroop battalion.

At Hervioux's command post, the situation was reviewed by grim and anxious men. The battle was not yet utterly lost and, with luck and help, the invaders might still be held. The most urgent needs were for artillery and small-arms ammunition. The radio crackled to Algiers. Help must come by dawn or the fortress would fall.

It rained that night — steady, driving rain, ice-cold. It soaked the little bands of defenders and closed off the skies with impenetrable darkness. All night the watchers strained for the sound of distant engines. Before dawn broke thinly on the crags, they knew no help would come.

As the skies lightened and cleared, *Luftwaffe* fighters took to the air to bomb and strafe villages, roads, and even isolated farmhouses. New flights of German gliders arrived laden with supplies and reinforcements. The rumble of heavy guns ringing the massif was a background for the crashing thunder of shells exploding within the fortress.

It was now brutally apparent that the Secret Army could not hold. And to prolong the losing battle would bring even more savage German reprisals against the civilian populace when the end came.

Time was needed to allow the defenders to break away.

Time was needed to evacuate forty seriously wounded men and women from the hospital. Time was needed to enable those civilians who could flee to make the attempt.

Hervioux ordered that the central Goulans Valley be held until night-fell. The man chosen to command this last stand was Léon Goderville, who had established the foundations of the fortress. He who had begun the battle two years earlier was now to finish it.

Group Goderville consisted of two companies of *maquis* and some regular army elements, including a detachment of Senegalese troops, about 350 men in all.

Chabal, the young lieutenant who had defended the Gorges of the Bourne on that first memorable attack months earlier, once again held a key position. Having echeloned his company along the winding track leading into the valley past the village of Valchevrière, he established his headquarters at the Belvédère.

Below him, Chabal could see the best part of a German motorized brigade. Elements of another brigade were attacking over the ridge on his right from Corrençon. German tanks and artillery were providing heavy fire support while Messerschmitts sprayed the narrow road with cannon and machine-gun fire.

At 7:00 A.M. the German motorized brigade attacked towards the Belvédère from Bois Barbeau, was halted, counterattacked, and thrown back to its starting line by a force less than a twentieth its strength. But the Germans attacked again and yet again. Through the bloody hours until 2:00 P.M. Company Chabal held them.

Chabal's men used every trick they knew. During a lull in the firing an Alsatian slipped into the German positions and began yelling, "New orders! The Americans have landed in Provence. We are to withdraw at once!" It was a transparent ruse, yet it caused enough confusion to delay the next assault for an hour or so.

By this time the enemy force attacking from Corrençon had scaled the ridge between the valleys and was behind Chabal. Goderville sent an urgent message ordering the lieutenant to retire. It could not be delivered because the battle had already reached the Belvédère. Chabal had time only to scribble the names of some of the wounded on a message sheet and stuff it in his pocket before his command post was overrun and he was shot. Weeks later the message was found on his body at the foot of the Belvédère cliff, over which the Germans had thrown not only the dead but the wounded as well.

Although Company Chabal was gone, Goderville's remaining men fought on to such effect that, when dusk began to shadow the sombre forests, Goulans was still free of Germans.

The day had seen many valorous deeds. Time after time the reinforced SS brigade at Vassieux had tried to break out of its encirclement and been thrown back. At the Pas de l'Aiguille in the southwest, Lieutenant Marcel Blanc and twenty-six survivors of his company fortified a cave from which they defied two battalions of German alpine troops throughout the day. They held the pass until the last of them was destroyed by charges of dynamite thrust into the cave on the ends of long poles.

From their positions high in the mountains in the north-west of the massif, Capitaine Duffans's *maquis* continued to pin down two battalions of German infantry.

Despite overwhelming superiority in numbers and fire-power, the Germans gained only minimal military success that day — and thereby lost their chance to annihilate the defenders of Vercors.

At 4:00 P.M. Hervioux gave the order to break contact and take to the mountains.

As he left his command post, which was already obscured by the smoke of burning documents, he was seen to be weep-ing openly. Victory had been so near. Had Vercors been granted just one more week of preparation, its defenders could — and almost certainly would — have thrown the Germans out.

By mid-morning the enemy held all the valleys of Vercors. They had captured the heart of the fortress . . . but in the high mountains and rain-swept forests, bands of desperately weary men were readying themselves to carry on the war.

The aftermath was frightful. Some three hundred men and women of the Secret Army had already been killed; now *more than four hundred civilians* — men, women, and children — were added to the death toll.

M. l'Abbé Gagnol was one of the few residents of Vassieux

to survive. He prepared a carefully documented report of what ensued. Here are some excerpts from it.

On July 21 M. Berthet, age 50, *citoyen* of Vassieux, took his eight-year-old daughter and hid with her in a small cave. When S.S. troops found his hiding place, Berthet identified himself and his child and came out to surrender. The German non-com replied, "You are terrorists!" and the man and his daughter were shot. . . .

Three children, ages four, five, and eight, ran from a burning house where their parents were dying and hid under a projecting ledge of rock. There they were discovered by the Germans, who lobbed a grenade amongst them, seriously wounding all three. . . .

Sixteen-year-old Marius Appaid was shot dead in front of his mother while she pleaded with the Germans to kill her instead. "You are too old and useless," was the contemptuous reply. . . .

Two wounded men of the airport construction group were strung up by their thumbs at each end of a single rope flung over a beam. The arrangement was such that the struggles of one produced intolerable agony for the other. They were left hanging until they died. . . .

The Fermond family, consisting of three adults and three

children, were burned to death in their own home by an S.S. detachment which threw phosphorus grenades through the windows. . . .

M. Jean Blanc, his sister, his grandparents, three of his daughters, and four other children who had taken refuge in his house were burned to death while the S.S. troops stood by with machine-pistols to prevent escape. Two days later the sole survivor, a terribly burned four-year-old, was found trapped in the ruins by Abbé Gagnol. When he called to her, "Where are the others, my child?" she answered feebly, "Mama lies on my feet, and Auntie will not move." The child died of her burns three days later. . . .

On July 25, in the nearby village of La Chapelle, all men and boys were herded into a house for "interrogation." During the night the women heard sustained bursts of firing. In the morning they were shown the slaughtered bodies of their male kinsfolk. . . .

———————————————————

Abbé Gagnol's list by no means exhausts the roster of atrocities. Of the 150 houses in the Vassieux area, the Germans destroyed 140 by fire or high explosives. For weeks afterwards the odour of putrefying flesh was so bad that some survivors could not force themselves to search the ruins.

In Villard-de-Lans, all remaining men were seized and

taken to Grenoble. There, on August 14, less than a week before the Allied liberation of that city, twenty were shot. The rest were shipped to concentration camps in Germany.

Throughout the whole of the Vercors, farmhouses that might have sheltered the defenders were destroyed.

At Saint-Nizier, twenty-six captured soldiers, most of them wounded, were condemned by a German court martial and shot, despite the fact that they were regular French army men in proper uniform.

Horror does not necessarily gain by repetition but one more incident, related by Tenant, deserves remembrance.

When the decision to break off the battle was made, the military hospital was evacuated to a cave called Grotte de la Luire in the southwest mountains. Thirty-six seriously wounded men, including four German prisoners and Lieutenant Chester Myers of the U.S. Rangers, were carried into the grotto. With them went doctors Fischer, Gannymede, and Ullmann, together with nine male nurses, two wounded women from Villard, and a priest, the R.P. de Montcheutil.

They knew they could not escape eventual detection and, in any case, the badly wounded needed hospital care, which as prisoners of war they would be entitled to receive. The retreat to the cave had been intended only to get the wounded and the non-combatants out of the line of fire until the heat of battle had dispersed. Dr. Fischer painted a huge red cross on the rocks in front of the cave, traces of which were still visible when I visited the place. There were no drugs and few bandages, but morale was high.

On July 27 a Messerschmitt circled the gorge, spotted the cross, and machine-gunned the mouth of the cave. This was a bad omen, but there was nothing to do except wait and hope. In the afternoon of July 30, one of the male nurses raced into the cave shouting, "*Les voilà!*"

A section of storm troopers appeared in the mouth of the cave. Without speaking, they raised machine pistols and began spraying the interior with fire while, behind them, the red cross flamed in the afternoon sun.

It was the German prisoners who prevented the massacre from being completed then and there. Their frantic cries were heard by an SS *Unteroffizier* who halted the shooting. The survivors were ordered out.

The shooting *might* have been a mistake. At least, this is what the wounded and the doctors hoped. They came out gladly, carrying the stretcher cases. Once outside the cave, those who could walk were marched off under guard, leaving the stretcher cases behind.

There were fourteen walking wounded. The Germans moved them to the edge of a ravine, then shot each one through the head. The bodies were dumped into the ravine, later to be doused with gasoline and burned. The stretcher cases were dealt with in similar fashion.

Meanwhile, the remainder had been herded to a nearby

road where Lieutenant Myers, the priest, the medical personnel, and the two women were loaded into a truck. The rest, including Lieutenant Dillon of the French Air Force who had been parachuted into Vercors, were shot.

Although all the wounded combatants were now dead except for Lieutenant Myers, the butchers were not satiated. Two days later, at Grenoble, Doctors Ullmann and Fischer and the priest were murdered. The male nurses were shipped to Ravensbrück, there to find death more slowly. Only Lieutenant Myers, Dr. Gannymede, and the two women survived to tell the story of the massacre at the Grotte de la Luire. It was a deed that set its mark on Vercors, a shadow hovering over those high mountains and green plains and clouding the memories of the survivors.

Fighting guerrilla actions whenever opportunity permitted, Hervieux's men maintained themselves in the mountain forests. As the Allies, striking up from south France and inland from Normandy, drew closer, the Germans began to withdraw and by the middle of August, Vercors was finally free of them for good.

———————————————

During the week I spent travelling around Vercors, Fran mostly remained at the hotel. This may have been as well. One evening, after returning from Vassieux, I started to tell her about some of the atrocities the Germans had perpetrated there, and she stopped me.

"I don't want to hear any more. When we came, this place seemed so lovely . . . so peaceful. Now it feels like a beautiful cemetery."

It was time to go, but now that I knew something of the story I felt compelled to pay one last visit to the Belvédère.

En route, I stopped beside a sturdy, middle-aged fellow accompanied by a teenage youth, both clad in workman's blue. I offered them a ride and they climbed in. The man identified himself as a stonemason, and the boy as his nephew and apprentice. This day being a holiday, they had set off to look for snails and mushrooms.

At their suggestion I stopped short of the Belvédère and joined them in their quest. Huge snails oozed along the dripping face of a roadside cliff, and mushrooms of kinds unknown to me erupted from the floor of the fringing pine forest. After collecting a bucket of each, we returned to the car and drove on to the Belvédère. By then it was late afternoon and the slim metal cross was throwing its shadow into the gorge as if pointing to the cluster of ruined buildings far below.

My companions would not leave the car and seemed anxious to be homeward-bound. When I suggested that they accompany me down the guttered track to the ruined village, the mason was vehement in his refusal.

"Nobody goes there! Nobody wants to remember those

things!" He paused and glanced at the cross. "For me, I wish it had all happened a thousand years ago!"

I drove them back to Viliard-de-Lans where they tried to give me half the snails and mushrooms. Before going to sleep on that last night in the Vercors, I thought about what the mason had said.

Perhaps, in a thousand years, Valchevrière *will* be forgotten.

Encounter at the Miramare

WE left Vercors in the morning, descending through the Gorges d'Engins to Grenoble, which spreads over a triangle of flood plain between three mountain massifs. The old provincial city looked pleasantly relaxed and inviting but we were anxious to put Vercors behind us, if we could not put it out of mind.

After some hours of driving south on the old Route Napoléon, skirting the Hautes-Alpes, we crossed the watershed and the character of the country changed. Warm colours — rich browns and ochreous reds — suffused the high slopes. Pine forests disappeared to be replaced by oaks and arid-climate trees. Fortresses and citadels of great age brooded over narrow valleys between dry and barren mountains. The streams changed too, becoming broad and shallow and, in many places, reduced to disconnected pools drying amongst stark, white mounds of gravel. Narrow gorges led us into and over steep cols, each more desert like than its predecessor.

Indulging my penchant for byways, we diverted to the Route des Alpes and climbed some five thousand feet into the mountainous and desiccated wilderness of Haute-Provence.

Driving was hard and tiring. When, at five o'clock, we entered the little town of Puget-Théniers, we were glad to call a halt.

The one hotel was haphazardly run by a fat and frowsty Madame of good will, if dubious appearance. We drank too much of her cognac, ate too much lamb stew (it had another and more palatable name in French), and went to bed in an alcove of a room overlooking a turgid stream. Thirst plagued me, and the stream must have sensed my plight for it grew active in the early hours, gurgling tantalizingly until I could bear it no longer. I stumbled out into the dawn in search of water.

The only other early wakers were knots of workmen on their way to the vineyards, and an ancient crone pulling a baby carriage stacked with firewood. When I asked her where I might get a drink she looked at me for a long, hostile moment before pointing to the passing stream whose green and oily waters were all too obviously laden with sewage. Eventually, I found a bistro just opening. A wan slattern who had been list-lessly sweeping the stone floors produced a bottle of mineral water and I was saved.

Experiencing no great desire to linger in Puget-Théniers, we descended towards the Mediterranean through the Var Valley, stopping occasionally to pick cherries from roadside trees. Palms and cacti began appearing, and with them white suburban villas. Soon we reached the outskirts of Nice, and the shores of the ancient Middle Sea.

We drove east along the famous Esplanade, gawking at gingerbread summer palaces, grandiose hotels, and semi-nude figures sprawled upon the beach. When I suggested that the latter looked like slightly underdone casualties of a nuclear explosion, Fran reproved me. "I'm sure they're all very nice people. You shouldn't make fun of them. It's not their fault they don't have enough to do."

In the eastern outskirts of the city we came upon an out-door service being conducted in memory of those who had died in the Resistance. Squads of gendarmes and platoons of regular soldiers stood at the salute as half a hundred Resistance veterans in civilian clothes laid wreaths and flowers on a monument newly cut out of the living rock of the cliff face. The only onlookers were ourselves and a few score working-class people dressed in black or wearing black brassards. I thought to myself that the sunbathers on the beach might have found something meritorious to do this day if they had tried.

A shimmering haze obscured the Mediterranean horizon as we followed the coastal highway eastward. Flaming vines clung to rock cuts and tropical flowers waxed in orgiastic display amongst the cactus phalli. We raced through Monaco and on to Menton, where smiling Italian customs officers waved us into their country.

Although this was still the Riviera of arid mountains crowding to the edge of the sea, it lacked the fringe of luxurious living characteristic of the French coast. Drab little towns clustered around cement plants and tile factories. Esplanades were either absent or dilapidated.

The day was drawing on and I was feeling lazy by the time we came to the town of Diano Marina. Spotting a garish purple *Albergo* sign on a villa facing a deserted and unkempt esplanade, I turned in on impulse.

The Miramare Hotel was unprepossessing: a stucco box with a discoloured pink façade. We went inside and found nobody in a barren foyer. I hallooed once or twice. Still nothing. As we were turning to leave, a door burst open and we were immersed in a flood of femininity.

Actually, there were only three of them but they made enough fuss for a dozen. One was large, black of hair and eye, with a formidable moustache. The second was a lean, dark little *siciliana* who looked as if inner fires were consuming her. The third was a tubby blonde with unkempt hair and murky eyes. They surrounded us spouting an incomprehensible mixture of Italian, French, a little English, and a little German.

It appeared that the Miramare had just opened for the summer, and we were the first customers. When I managed to break into the torrent long enough to ask for a room and dinner, all hell broke loose. It seemed there were nine rooms to let and each of the ladies had her own opinion as to which one should be ours. The *siciliana* demanded we be put in Number Seven. Moustache thundered that it must be Number Four. Blondie simpered that Number One would be more appropriate.

To avoid being embroiled in what threatened to become a donnybrook, we picked up our bags and fled up a flight of dusty marble stairs to the second floor, where we selected a room that overlooked the sea and contained two single beds. We had barely put down our bags before the *siciliana* burst in, snatched them up, and raced down the hall to fling them on an enormous double bed in Number Seven. This done, she fixed me with a glittering eye and launched into a tirade, the gist of which was that *I* could not fool *her*. *I* was no ordinary tourist. I was an *inglese* priest having a fling with his lady love!

She broke into a radiant smile and added, "I am a good Catholic girl but I believe in love! And you poor priests . . . better you sleep with a real woman than an altar boy!"

I could think of no better reply than to give her a conspiratorial wink, whereupon she screamed with delight and hared off to tell the other ladies. As we unpacked, we could hear shrieks of merriment from below.

The evening being young, we went for a walk. The sea looked clean and the beach inviting. We bought bathing suits at a little clothing shop, changed behind some crumbling concrete fortifications, and went for a swim. The water was glorious, but we did not enjoy it long. Howls rent the air as the *siciliana* came racing along the esplanade, waving her arms wildly.

"*Minato! Minato!*" she was screaming. "*Pericolo! Pericolo!* Papa, you going to *die!*"

I knew about *minato*. With heart in mouth, I led Fran out of the water and we tiptoed across the beach, carefully stepping in our own footprints. We now had an explanation for the empty beaches and esplanades we had so far encountered in Italy. They had been sown with anti-personnel mines to deter Allied commando raids.

Our dark saviour shepherded us back to the hotel, where we were crushingly embraced by all three ladies, congratulated on our miraculous escape, and plied with glasses of a murky substance that tasted like prunes but had the kick of a kangaroo.

As we were dressing we heard a car screech to a stop outside. I peered over the balcony and saw a beetle-green MG disgorging a dust-covered, dungaree-clad young couple. Somehow, I knew they were Canadians so I went down to greet them. They had paused only to find a toilet, but I prevailed upon them to stay the night.

"You will not," I assured them, "find another hotel like the Miramare."

Dinner was a Miramare event. As the four of us consulted

a laboriously handwritten menu and selected each course, the *siciliana* relayed our decisions to Moustache, who was the cook. She, in turn, barked orders to Blondie, who jumped on a bicycle and wheeled off to, I suppose, the nearest market.

This routine was repeated with every course, which made for long intervals between servings. We filled these with wine and conversation. Peter and Deborah, our new acquaintances, were from Montreal, newly married, and spending their two-week honeymoon seeing Europe. They were wasting no time about it, either. On this particular day, they had crossed half of Spain, traversed southern France into Italy and, had we not distracted them, might have been well into Switzerland before quitting time. They told us they had slept the previous night in a Spanish desert, wakening to find their sleeping bag crawling with adventurous scorpions. They preferred mountain roads, they said, not for the scenery but because the loops and curves gave Peter a better chance to improve his cornering techniques.

We found them delightful, if somewhat terrifying. Peter admitted to having an ulcer and Deborah to having a little trouble holding her water; otherwise they appeared to be almost unbearably robust. Young Argonauts of a new breed.

It was well after midnight before Fran and I staggered off to bed, leaving Peter and his bride dancing the tarantella to cymbal rhythms supplied by the *siciliana*, while Moustache belted out the tune on an old piano. Ah, to be young again at the Miramare.

My opportunity for a youthful fling came next morning when I was cornered outside the bathroom by the *siciliana*, with the urgent suggestion that she and I make a quick visit to Number Nine. I demurred, on the grounds that my "friend" and I had to be on our way. The lady skewered me with a hot glare of contempt.

"Pigs!" she spat. "All you Papas! Go back to your altar boys then!"

Eastward bound, I found it hard to rid myself of the notion that the little Hillman had become an MG racer. The Riviera di Ponente road clung precariously to rocky headlands, descending briefly into arid, dusty, red-tiled towns. We were not sorry to reach Genoa and head northward into the Po Valley.

Now the road became dead flat and straight, and my arm muscles began to relax. There was little traffic except for motorcycles, motor bicycles, and motor scooters that ran in shoals as unpredictable as schools of minnows.

We lunched in an ancient chapel that had taken on a new lease on life as a *ristorante*. We ate veal and drank beer under a vaulted ceiling decorated with cherubim and armorial plaques, while the proprietor, an ex-Italian navy man, told us what it had felt like to be sunk by a *British* destroyer.

Travelling with the top down, we got too much sun and were glad to see Pavia looming in the distance, looking cool and quiet on its low hills. It proved to be neither. We had to fight our way through enormous throngs that had taken over all the thoroughfares for the Sabbath promenade. We were able to force our way through the narrow, airless streets only by using the horn constantly and sometimes administering bumper nudges to clots of pedestrians. Fortunately, the townsfolk were in high good humour and tolerated our boorishness.

Early next day we reached Milan, where we sought out a young Austrian who ran the literary agency handling my work in Italy.

Leopold took us to an outdoor café for lunch and told us wild and woolly yarns of his wartime experiences. Being Austrian and Jewish, he had made for France after the *anschluss*. When France fell he slipped away to Italy, but had to flee again to Switzerland, where he was interned. Towards the end of the war, he returned to Italy and became an interpreter for the Germans while, according to him, acting as a spy for the Allies. Growing bored he crossed the lines to become an officer in the U.S. Army O.S.S.

I harboured some suspicions about his story but admired his histrionic storytelling. He even managed to persuade me that the several thousand lira he had received as an advance payment on royalties for *People of the Deer* could not be paid to me in Italy because of some obscure legal requirement. I concluded that he would go far in his new profession.

By mid-afternoon we had put Milan behind us and were rolling down the long, hot, dusty road that angles east along the base of the Apennines towards the Adriatic. We now had to share the highway with herds of huge diesel tractor-trailers. Their drivers, known as *Komerads* (not to be mistaken for party members), seemed a jovial, if unshaven lot and courteous to small red Hillmans.

Near Parma we stopped at a brand-new roadside hotel. Here, for the first time in Europe, we had a bathroom to ourselves but, Italian-style, there was no running water. And we were awakened at midnight by several hundred thousand young Germans from a bus tour marching up and down the halls. They were back on duty again at 3:00 A.M.

We were seeing more and more German tourists driving shiny new Porsches and Volkswagens, and looking much more prosperous than their French, Italian, or English counterparts. It seemed peculiar to find them swarming so abundantly in places where they had made their mark for barbarism only a few short years ago.

Next day we followed the highway a few miles past Bologna then struck off eastwards on a dirt track through a patchwork of little farms in dead-flat country. We were now driving along the same roads the German army had used when it defended this region against the advancing First Canadian Division in 1944.

The small town of Russi appeared amongst olive trees and vineyards and we drove through its dusty main street into the civic square. It was empty except for a colossal marble aircraft wing set on end, shadowing a larger-than-life bronze aviator with arms akimbo and out-thrust chin, Mussolini-style. A plaque on the base informed us that this impressive monument was in honour of Italian fliers killed in Ethiopia. Shell fragments had chipped and pocked the sixty-foot-high wing and pigeons had whitened its soaring tip. It seemed so out of place in this remote little community that we could not imagine what feat of political legerdemain could have planted it here.

Although Russi had suffered our gunfire for months, I was amazed at how little apparent damage had been inflicted. Only after Fran remarked that the houses looked surprisingly new did I twig. Almost all had been completely rebuilt, on their original foundations, out of original stones, and in the old style.

The Italian *paesani* had wrought a miracle here in one of the most viciously fought-over battlefields of the war. Furthermore, the work of restoration had been done with their own hands and with little or no assistance from government or reconstruction agencies. Not only had they restored the buildings; they had done the same with the surrounding farms, vineyards, and orchards, all of which had been devastated by the engines of war.

We drove on to cross the Senio River into Bagnacavallo, in whose ruined houses I and my companions had sought shelter from shells, freezing rain, and the imminence of death during Christmas week of 1944.

A small hotel overlooking the central square seemed vaguely familiar. We parked Liz and pushed aside beaded fly curtains to enter the ground-floor *ristorante*. This dark and cavernous room was marvellously cool and silent, except for the buzzing of a bluebottle. An old man emerged from a back room to serve us sticky glasses of Marsala.

"You seem really far away," Fran murmured as we sipped the strong sweet wine.

"I've been in this room before," I said, "only then the front was smashed open, so my driver was able to park the jeep in here. One night a Jerry shell came through the roof, failed to explode, and bounced down three flights of stairs to whomp into the driver's seat. Which was where we found it in the morning."

It may have been the Marsala. Or perhaps it was the white heat shimmering off the walls of Bagnacavallo. Or it may have been the odour of urine, wine lees, cooking oil, and dust — the "burnt umber" smell of small Italian towns. Whatever. The floodgates of memory were swinging open, releasing a deluge of recollections.

The old proprietor gave us a cool room on the second floor and a bed with a feather tick, and there we spent the night. But I did not sleep well. I had been here before.

Operation Chuckle

WINTER is not the time to do battle along the Adriatic coast of Italy. We Canadian foot soldiers had learned this the hard way during the winter of 1943. However, the high command had not learned it or, if they had, chose to ignore it. As December of 1944 approached, First Canadian Corps was ordered to "burst out" of the narrow corridor of coastal plain between mountains and sea, "sweep" north past Ravenna, and open the way for a triumphant advance by Eighth Army into the Po Valley. The staff officers at Allied Forces Headquarters who contrived this plan cheerfully code-named it Operation Chuckle.

First Division was to attack northwestward across three major rivers, several canals, and innumerable deep ditches draining reclaimed swampland. The major water courses ran between high embankments, some standing thirty feet above sodden orchards and vineyards. All were in spate and their waters, fed by mountain torrents, were bitterly cold. Each of these natural defence lines was manned by élite German troops, well dug in and well armed.

Chuckle began on December 2. By the third, the advance had stalled in front of the high-dyked Lamone River. The Hastings and Prince Edward Regiment was told to cross the river and seize a bridgehead on the other side.

The weather was atrocious. Rain, sleet, and snow were turning the countryside into a half-frozen quagmire. The infantry waded through it remembering that, in similar conditions a year and a day earlier, they had been moving into a bloodbath at the Moro River, 130 miles to the south.

Ten minutes before midnight Baker and Charlie, the two assault companies, reached their start line at the base of the massive Lamone dykes. From far to the rear they heard a sullen rumble as our guns began firing the barrage that was to precede the attack. Cliff Broad, Baker's commander and my close friend, was lying just below the crest of the near dyke. The familiar wail of shells from our medium guns rang in his ears . . . but then, instead of passing overhead to fall upon the enemy, they began falling on the dykes.

The earth shook and heaved and red and yellow flashes illuminated a charnel scene as shrapnel sliced through steel helmets, bones, and flesh. A biting white smoke added its special horror as phosphorous grenades hanging from men's belts were hit by shrapnel and exploded.

When the shelling ceased, the living lay immobile, stunned, in the awful silence of the aftermath. Then the cries of the wounded began to rise, a threnody of agony. Half the men of Baker were dead or wounded. Charlie, which had gone into battle with a strength of only two platoons, was now reduced to less than one.

The regiment should have been withdrawn after this débâcle. Instead, it was ordered to make the assault as planned.

Able and Dog companies plodded forward. A false dawn provided just enough light for them to avoid trampling their dead comrades below the dykes. Dog and Able managed to scramble across the river, scale the far bank, and dig themselves in.

They came under sustained and ferocious enemy bombardment. Then the Germans counter-attacked with infantry, self-propelled guns, and tanks. The tiny bridgehead began to shrink towards collapse. Reinforcements were urgently needed but the only available troops were what remained of Baker Company.

Cliff Broad took the forty or so survivors across the Lamone and into an attack that drove the surprised Germans back some three hundred yards. Baker's men then went to ground in the middle of a vineyard under a hail of mortar bombs and small-arms fire. Enemy tanks soon began to converge upon them. Nevertheless, they held until, by 9:00 A.M., it was clear that to remain where they were would be to die where they were.

Broad gave the order to get out. Under intense fire, dragging some of their wounded, the survivors scuttled to the river. Some drowned during the crossing. The remainder, joined by what was left of Able and Dog, tumbled over the crest of the near dyke and rolled heavily down its slope. They were back on the start line where, nine hours earlier, they had suffered a holocaust brought about by our own guns. The living had now rejoined the dead.

For five days thereafter the weather drew a shroud over the Lamone killing ground. Rain beat down unceasingly. The ground became so saturated that slit trenches filled as soon as they were dug. Wet snow splashed the wasteland that had once been neatly patterned vineyards and fields. The only shelter to be found — and it was minimal — was in scattered, stone farm buildings, but these were being steadily pulverized by German guns.

Relationships between soldiers and civilians grew closer. Since both shared a world of destruction, they began to share other things. Cans of bully beef found their way into pots of steamy pasta that nurtured *paesani* and *soldati* alike. An old woman took to mixing hot wine with the juice of a few scrofulous oranges to put heart into patrols that had to feel their way into the black, bullet-studded nights.

When the weather improved a little, the Lamone was crossed by other troops and shortly thereafter orders arrived for the regiment to fight its way forward to the Canale Naviglio.

Having had considerable experience with attacks on their dyke positions, the Germans knew the form. Mustering all their mortars and high-angle howitzers, they brought their fire to bear on the ground immediately behind the south dyke of the Naviglio. The crump of falling bombs and shells merged into an almost continuous roar as the forward companies prepared to attempt the crossing.

But our engineers had not yet managed to bridge the Lamone, and until they did so neither tanks nor anti-tank guns could reach us. An advance that would put yet *another* dyked barrier between us and these supporting arms seemed madness. Through the rest of the day we waited for news that the Lamone had been bridged and that supporting arms were moving forward. The news never came.

At 1800 hours the Commanding Officer, Lieutenant-Colonel Don Cameron, called an orders group. By then the pressure from divisional headquarters had mounted to the point where it could no longer be resisted. "Support or no support, we have to get on with it!" Cameron told his company commanders.

In the company areas men gathered their weapons with dull and fatalistic resignation. No one said the actual words, but each man heard them. "Here we go again." The mutter of distant guns and the crash of exploding shells became part of each man's heartbeat.

At 2200 hours the three assault companies scrambled across the Naviglio in a night hideous with the sounds of battle. Before dawn all three had reached their objectives.

Baker Company had the farthest to go — a little group of farmhouses called San Carlo, almost a thousand yards beyond the Naviglio. Good luck and surprise helped them reach it.

Charlie, in a supporting role, squelched its way to a point halfway between Baker and the canal, then tried to dig in.

Able struck out along the lateral road beneath the northern dyke and was soon fighting for possession of a row of farmhouses.

By dawn the scraps of news that were filtering back to battalion headquarters seemed good. However, Cameron could take no comfort from them until he knew the Lamone had been bridged and Sherman tanks were coming up.

Now the Germans struck back. The voice of Baker Company's signaller, distorted by static, echoed in Cameron's receiver.

"Counter-attack with tanks coming in from the left. . . . Another attack coming from the front with Mark IV tanks. . . . We have to have tank support or anti-tank guns. . . . They are closing in."

The voice of Major Stockdale, commanding the company, came on the air. "We can't hold out," he said. "Do you wish us to remain or withdraw?"

Cameron replied, "You must remain. . . ."

His decision was of the sort that ages men and withers their souls. Knowing that he was probably dooming Baker to destruction, he nevertheless could not allow it to withdraw. The sacrifice of Baker was needed to buy time until the Shermans could arrive.

Baker's radio went off the air.

Spread-eagled in the frigid mud, the men of Charlie Company watched helplessly as the Germans closed in on San Carlo. They watched Mark IV tanks methodically shatter each house in turn, reducing it to smoking rubble. Baker Company was gone.

Meanwhile, Able, holding houses along the dyke wall, had come under attack from two self-propelled guns and a strong force of infantry. Able's three depleted platoons were cut off from one another and two were forced back across the canal, leaving only Nine Platoon, reduced to fewer than a dozen men, to hold the position.

Now it was Charlie's turn. With the leisureliness of those who are assured of victory, the Germans turned on it. The men of Thirteen Platoon raised their heads during a lull in the bombardment to find themselves staring into the muzzles of German rifles and carbines. Thirteen Platoon vanished and, apart from two wounded men, was not heard of again.

The CO did what he could. What remained of Dog Company was ordered forward but, suffering from the effects of seven days of continuous shellfire and the loss of most of its officers and NCOs, it had lost heart. Three times it set out for the canal, and three times returned.

Battalion headquarters was in a large *casa* two or three hundred yards to the rear of the dykes. The padre described what it was like.

"From dawn until late afternoon the house was under constant bombardment — moaning Minnies, 88s, everything in the book came at us. Early on, a shed on the south side was demolished by a direct hit. There were a lot of casks of *vino* in the shed and a number of men had bedded down amongst them and were trying to rest. The casks were all perforated but most of the men miraculously escaped and ran into the main building, soaked in wine. The wine flowed across the floor behind them and for the rest of the day we lived in the sour stink of *vino* fumes.

"As time passed the building grew more and more crowded. The remnants of Able Company found shelter here, along with those of Dog Company. By this time the battle had begun to look like Armageddon for us. Only Charlie was left in front and the messages coming through were increasingly desperate. 'The enemy is pressing close.' 'We're running out of ammo.' 'What are your orders?'

"I would have defied anyone to tell what was passing through Cameron's mind as he quietly told the signaller to reply, 'Help is coming. Hold on.'

"Cameron's coolness steadied us though we were sure

the promise of relief was just a pipe dream. With enemy tanks crawling around a few hundred yards in front and capable of crossing the Naviglio whenever they wished, and remembering that behind us were two canals that, as far as we knew, had not yet been bridged and were impassable to our tanks, we couldn't see that we had much of a hope.

"Suddenly we heard the rumble of tank treads on the road outside. Our common thought was, 'Well, this is goodbye.'

"Then someone peered out a window and yelled, and we knew how the boys must have felt at the seige of Lucknow when they heard the skirl of the pipes. Coming up the road was a squadron of British Columbia Dragoon tanks, swinging their seventeen-pounder guns from side to side. We heard later that the first of the tanks had crossed the Lamone before the bolts on the bridge were even tight."

The Dragoons wasted no time. Finding a ford, the tanks rumbled over the Naviglio, firing as they went. One appeared outside the ruins of the house where the remnant of Charlie Company was making its final stand. As it nosed around the corner of the building it was hit by a German shell. The wounded gunner crawled out of the turret and some of Charlie's men raced out and dragged him under cover. All the gunner said was, "Did we make it in time?"

They had made it in time.

Early one afternoon, at a time when sensible people were letting their dinners digest and avoiding the heat of the day, Fran and I went in search of San Carlo. The map directed us along a track beside the now-shrunken Canale Naviglio, then northward to a cluster of white houses glistening in the sun.

We pulled into a courtyard flanked by spanking new buildings standing four-square under red-tiled roofs. If *this* was San Carlo, I thought, it had surely risen from the grave. I got out and stood uncertainly, waiting for a sign. All was motionless except for a garishly green lizard scampering across the neatly laid stone pavement.

Then a door opened and a slim young man came out. He advanced somewhat timidly for, though Fran and I could not know it, we were the first foreigners to come here since the war.

"*Si, signore,*" he replied in answer to my question. "This is San Carlo and you and the *signora,*" he smiled at Fran, "are very welcome to Casa Balardini. Please to come in."

We were received in the cool, dark room reserved for celebrations. Roused from their naps by a stentorian cry from the *maestro,* Signore Balardini, a big man with straggling moustaches and a belly that gave him presence, the rest of the family came stumbling, running, and striding into the room.

There seemed to be no end to them, spanning several generations. They clustered around us, touching our shoulders, smiling, laughing, and bombarding us with questions.

We were being treated as honoured guests, but I was uneasy.

How were these people going to react when they realized I was one of the *soldati canadesi* whose guns had also contributed to the devastation of San Carlo?

I need not have worried. A middle-aged man thrust a glass of wine into my hand.

"*Canadese, no*? I am captured by you boys in Sicily in 1943. I work for your engineers. They put me in *canadese* uniform and I learn to speak English good. *Canadese molto bene!*"

Relieved, I explained who we were and what we were doing. Far from souring the mood, this seemed to warm it even more. However, if the Balardinis harboured no resentment towards us, their feelings towards the *tedeschi*, as most Italians called the Germans, were another matter.

"When you kick the goddamned *tedeschi* out of here that time everything gets smashed. Too bad! But it don't matter so long you got those Nazi bastards out. We can fix everything so long we are free from those sons of bitching fascists!"

The sentiments of this fervent little speech, repeated in Italian, were vehemently confirmed by the family, who now seemed intent on making us one with them.

Frances, who had edged to the door to get some breathing space, was now frantically waving at me. "They're taking the luggage out of the car!" she cried.

They were indeed, it having apparently been decided we were moving in to Casa Balardini. Only with great difficulty was I able to convince them we could not stay the night. There was, however, no gainsaying their demand that we eat with them before travelling on.

While the women rushed off to prepare the meal, the men and children proudly escorted us around the farm. It embraced just three acres, and everything that had stood or grown on this small piece of earth had been virtually obliterated during the winter of 1944. Now the land had come alive again. Grapes were forming on neat rows of vines. Young orchards were thriving, and peaches and cherries were already ripe. One supple lad swarmed up a tree and showered us with firm-fleshed fruit.

Every inch of soil was in use. Corn grew between the vines and in the aisles between fruit trees. Cabbages, tomatoes, eggplants, and other vegetables flourished between the rows of corn. Narrow strips of wheat crowded to the very edge of the road. There were no weeds on the Balardini farm — there was no room for them. Cows, mules, pigs, goats, chickens, and ducks lived in and around the outbuildings. The place was a living supermarket — as it had to be in order to support so many human mouths.

Late that afternoon we sampled its produce. The dishes were too many to remember but I know we ate chicken and kid with a dozen different vegetables and filled our plates from countless pasta dishes redolent of herbs, spices, and sharp white cheese. Wine flowed freely.

Not until we had eaten and drunk rather more than our fill did the talk turn to the December day when Operation

Chuckle sent Baker Company to Casa Balardini.

Deprived of most of its men by military service and German labour round-ups, what remained of the family had taken refuge in the cellars.

"There were only about thirty *canadesi* here," we were told, "then whole companies of *tedeschi* with many *carri armati* [tanks and mobile guns] surrounded the *casa* and blew it to pieces, room by room. The noise was so bad our one remaining pig burst out of its sty and ran right towards a tank, and the *tedeschi* shot it with machine guns. . . . Everything that moved got shot. You could smell blood everywhere. . . . My cousin Maria turned eight the day before the battle; a big girl but thin because there was so little food. She must have been too hungry to think straight. She sneaked out to what was left of the vegetable garden. Then the shells came and she just disappeared. Later we found her feet and one arm. . . . Some of the shells had phosphorus inside them and when they exploded everything was sprayed with fire. Water wouldn't put it out. My aunt was hit by a piece of that stuff and it burned a hole right into her belly. A Canadian soldier bound it up but she died anyway, screaming and screaming."

As the German assault grew fiercer, the surviving Balardinis huddled in a stinking vault below the cattle stable. A salvo of shells brought the roof down and the walls tumbled in. One old man was killed and a young woman suffered a crushed thigh. The cattle were all killed.

After overrunning the farm, the Germans herded the few surviving Canadians (the Balardinis thought there were no more than ten) into captivity but did not discover the Italians in their hole. The survivors emerged two days later to find the destruction so complete they had to abandon the place and seek refuge with relatives beyond Bagnacavallo.

"When we came back," the oldest woman told us, "we found everything broken or gone, and the next winter was hard. We lived through it. We went to work. And now . . ." she gave me a gap-toothed grin ". . . well, *here we are!*"

It was late when, laden with gifts of wine and fruit, we left San Carlo. I also took with me a souvenir of a different kind — a shell fragment from a great heap that had been collected from the fields during cultivation — a harvest of steel.

Ortona

WE had arranged to meet an Italian writer in Ravenna, but when we reached that ancient city he was nowhere to be found, so we drove south to a *pensione* in the seaside village of Cervia, and had a swim in the somewhat soupy waters of the Adriatic.

Next morning we returned to the "front," following the old Eighth Army supply route, code-named Sun-Up. It had led to sundown for many good men. We passed through miles of open pine plantations where Byron had once wandered, and I had looked for birds in moments stolen from the war.

Turning inland along a farm track, we found the Bailey bridges our engineers had erected over the canals still in place; they were rusted a bit, but usable. The surrounding fields seemed to close in upon us so lushly we felt claustrophobic. Where once had been only muddy desolation was now a near-tropical growth of vines, crops, and trees.

We made our way to a long, barn-like *casa* that had been the headquarters of First Brigade, and of the brigadier many held responsible for the dreadful débâcle at the Lamone. Here, two days after that battle, Lieutenant Joe Naylor and I may have saved the brigadier's life.

We were standing outside the building when we heard angry voices and saw two muddy figures carrying Tommy guns reeling towards us through the night. They asked where the brigadier was. Joe recognized them as survivors of Dog Company. There was no doubt as to what they had in mind, and it took a lot of persuasion to get them headed back to the regiment's lines. To tell the truth, we were not concerned about the brigadier — we simply did not want these two good men to have to face a firing squad.

Late in the day Fran and I made our way back to Cervia. In our absence, a blond German couple had arrived at the *pensione*. The man had been an *Oberstleutnant* (lieutenant-colonel) in the élite First Paratroop Division. He, too, was revisiting scenes of battle. When I admitted to having been a soldier in the same theatre, he became very friendly.

"*Ach*, then, we are comrades-in-arms," he said warmly.

"Not exactly. We fought on different sides and for different reasons, I believe."

He shrugged. "What matter? Good soldiers obey orders, do they not? It was not for us to say if an order is right or wrong. You Canadians fought very well. It is an honour to meet you."

He made no effort to conceal the fact that he had been a member of the Nazi party. "I am not now, of course, but in Germany one had no choice if one desired a military career." He smiled engagingly. "Mistakes were made, but that is, how do you say, *Wasser unter* the bridge, no? We must drink together. I have brought with me some good schnapps."

Frances and I excused ourselves and went to bed. She was relieved. "You looked," she said as we got undressed, "as if you were going to sink your teeth into his throat. You really should learn to conceal your feelings better."

We drove south to Rimini over more of the walled canals that had been such obstacles to us during the winter battles. Rimini was so jammed with people it was impossible to move except in fits and starts. A carnival spirit was in the air and we soon learned why. A round-Italy bicycle race was due to pass through town in a few hours and everyone for miles around had gathered to cheer on their favourites. Long-distance bicycle races are amongst the most popular of Italian sports, but they play the devil with road traffic.

Not far inland, Monte Titano signalled the presence of the Most Serene Republic of San Marino. Concluding that the steepness of its approach road would discourage bicycles, we headed towards it.

The road climbed through massive, rounded hills covered with vineyards, until Titano reared above us like a titanic medieval castle complete with crazily crenellated battlements. Together with its attendant mountains, it forms a massif, similar in some respects to that of Vercors though much smaller.

The town, and capital, of San Marino clings to a pinnacle in the centre of the massif. It is a place of narrow, cobbled streets and ancient, huddled houses of undressed stone over which five Catholic churches preside possessively. Three smaller communities cluster around decaying fortresses on the surrounding bastions of the massif.

One of, if not *the*, world's smallest independent states, San Marino embraces twenty-four square miles of peaks and valleys with a population of about twelve thousand people and as many hardy upland cattle. It is a political anomaly. When first mentioned in history, in the fourth century, it was but one of a myriad of little states in the patchwork that would eventually coalesce to become Italy. San Marino avoided being incorporated into the national quilt for reasons not entirely clear, but probably because none of its neighbours coveted it. On the other hand, none of them wanted anyone else to have it. So, in the end, all agreed to leave it alone.

It is an odd sort of republic, governed by a council, or parliament, of sixty members, one-third being "nobles," one-third urban burgesses, and one-third rural landowners. All are chosen by the council itself, thereby dispensing with such nonsense as elections. There is an *opera buffa* army, and a professional bureaucracy well versed in how to look after itself.

We had lunch on the terrace of an eagle's eyrie of a *ristorante*. Only some excellent Orvieto wine, served by a luscious dark-eyed wench, kept me from getting vertigo whenever I looked out over empty space towards the distant sapphire of the Adriatic.

I struck up a conversation with a slick-haired fellow in a Mafia-style suit who turned out to be the law courts recorder and learned from him that San Marino was no place for a writer. It had no printing press.

Ah well . . . I also learned that San Marino was a Socialist Republic or, to put it more bluntly, communist. Well, sort of. Since the state's income came mostly from gambling, smuggling, providing sanctuary for corporations of dubious repute, and the sale of postage stamps, perhaps communist-capitalist would better describe it. Occasionally, Sanmarinese may remember they are red comrades in an international confederacy — but I suspect they don't do that very often.

Having stocked up on tax-free cigarettes, we returned to Italy and the coast, and again turned southward, encountering almost no other cars except a scattering of shiny, new Volkswagens with Deutschland licence plates. By way of contrast, a few farm carts rolled along on the wheels and tires of long-defunct army vehicles.

That evening we looked up an old comrade of mine in

San Benedetto del Tronto. Late in 1943 Giovanni Tarborelli, one-time captain in the Cremona Division of the Italian Army, was seconded to First Canadian Brigade as an interpreter. He and I worked together through the next several months and became friends. Now he did the Italian thing. For two days and most of two nights we were escorted around town and countryside, meeting innumerable relatives and being fêted with enormous meals and saturated with the best of the excellent local wines.

Sometimes we drank coffee or an aperitif at a table outside one of the five cafés ringing the town's *piazza*. Each was the headquarters of a different political party, and ferocious glares and barbed comments were freely traded across the square. Although it seemed likely we would find ourselves caught in the middle of a local war, no violence ensued. Communists and Christian Democrats seemed to be the major parties. Giovanni favoured socialism, but thought it likely the Communists would win the forthcoming election. The possibility did not distress him.

"If it's a choice between the old right-wing parties — the ones who ran Garibaldi's beautiful Italy into the ground and nearly into the grave — I would take the Communists. Those of us who have lived under a dictatorship of the right have no illusions."

We were impressed by the optimism and energy of the San Benedetto people. Apparently the more a family had lost because of the war, the greater and more vigorous their efforts to build anew.

An exception was the urbane scion of a ducal family that had once owned most of the arable land around San Benedetto. The war had reduced him to living with only five servants in a cramped little *castello* containing no more than forty rooms. He complained of the deprivations he was forced to endure, which, he told us, would become much worse if the Bolsheviks came to power. For him, the future was overcast with gloom.

It was quite the opposite with a peasant family we visited later that same day. Like the Balardinis, these people had lost everything. Their small patch of land had been devastated, first by German and then by British troops using it as an assembly area for tanks and heavy transport. Their buildings had been demolished when Royal Air Force fighter-bombers attacked the German vehicle park. Three of the men in the family had been killed in action in north Africa and another by the Germans in Italy after being accused of helping the local partisans. And yet not only had they managed to rebuild and restore most of the material things they had lost, they were filled with enthusiasm for the future.

"They believe," Giovanni explained, "that the time of the little people has come at last. And I believe it."

We drank to that.

"But the Black Shirts are not gone," he warned us. "They will fight to return in one form or another, and with the help of the mafia of the big businessmen, the old landowners, the banks, and the church, try to push us back into poverty. Only *this* time we will not let them!"

We drank to that, too.

The hot, dry weather ended abruptly on our last night in San Benedetto. The skies opened and rain drenched the land. Dry-as-dust *torrenti* became *fiumane*, springing to watery life and roaring and foaming on their way to the sea. In the morning when we headed on south, one could almost hear the vegetation sucking up the moisture.

Our next destination was the small coastal city of Ortona, in and around which, during the winter of 1943–44, we fought the bloodiest battles of our war in Italy.

The highway continued to hug the coast and we continued to play tag with big trucks, which seemed to become ever more numerous the farther south we drove. Ortona loomed ahead on a great headland from which its high walled fortress had dominated the coast since ancient times.

Between us, we and the Germans succeeded in reducing this city of twenty thousand people to a jumble of rubble. Even though an enormous amount of restoration had been done since war's end, the wounds were by no means healed. None of Ortona's hotels had yet been rendered habitable so we backtracked up the coast to the one-time seaside resort of Francavilla. It, too, had been terribly damaged but we found a room in a *pensione*.

After lunch we drove back through Ortona to the Moro River Military Cemetery. Fourteen hundred men of First Canadian Division lie here in incomparable surroundings on a high point overlooking the Adriatic. Amongst them is Major Alex Campbell, once my company commander. Alex, an indomitable mountain of a man, was killed on Christmas Day 1943. His father had died in battle with the Kaiser's Germans on Christmas Day 1916.

We poked about old battlefields for the next few days. I found it deeply disturbing, not in ways I had anticipated, but because the transformation of hideously familiar scenes into lush, even pretty glimpses of an alien Eden seemed to mock what had happened to me and my companions here. These wanderings near Ortona brought me no solace.

One morning Fran and I visited an advanced observation post where I had spent some of the most terror-filled hours of my life being sniped at by a German 88mm gun. The farmer who owned the land walked over to pass the time of day. He offered a drink from a straw-covered bottle, but even as I sipped the wine my ears were tautly attuned for the shriek and whistle of an incoming shell.

We went inland along the San Leonardo track, which in our time had been the main highway for an army. Beyond Dundee Crossroads we came to the gully where Doc McConnell, my batman, dug me the most luxurious foxhole of any war — but forgot to take into account the cumulative effect of ceaseless rain, which brought it all down on my sleeping head one night.

I had another memory of this gully.

Early in January of 1944 the sun briefly returned and the shell-churned ground began to thaw. During a lull I went for a cautious walk and unexpectedly came upon an old woman prodding the ground with a brass rod from a bedstead. She had no business being there, for all civilians had been evacuated, or so we thought. I questioned her.

During that ghastly winter she had remained in hiding in an abandoned German dugout. For company she had had her daughter and granddaughter — both of whom had died well before the new year began. For three months this old woman had endured in a muddy cave, emerging to grub for roots and anything else edible, while waiting for the ground to thaw sufficiently so she could bury her dead.

I could tolerate the revival of no more such memories, so we departed from Ortona, heading south. We had not driven far before entering a world where no vestiges of the war were to be seen. The weight of sick remembrance began to ease. Stopping by the roadside we picked green figs and looked at birds — a jay, some skylarks, and a soaring kite. My mood lightened as we pressed on, even though the countryside became more and more impoverished, the *casas* smaller, meaner, and more dispersed over a sun-bleached landscape.

At Termoli we turned our backs on the Adriatic and headed inland. We were for the mountains now. The gravel road that would take us across the Apennines was under repair and barely passable. Loads of rocks had been dumped at intervals along its verges and on each perched a weathered-looking fellow with a sledgehammer and a bottle of *vino*. Those road menders evidently sympathized with what we were enduring for they waved their bottles encouragingly as we jolted past.

As we got closer to the mountains, the road began an endless zigzag climb. We lunched beside a dry *torrente* on bread, bone-hard sausages, and goat's cheese bought at a little shop in Vasto, and were entertained by a small boy with a bull calf.

Appearing out of nowhere this child spent the next hour leading his rambunctious charge up and down a quarter-mile stretch of road, to no apparent purpose. Eventually we twigged. He was schooling the calf to traffic (a total of one Vespa and two old trucks rattled by while we were there), in preparation for its future life as a draft animal. School over, the pair went off to swim in a pothole in the riverbed.

As we climbed higher, the slopes appeared to be adorned with clusters of pearl shell — the white-washed façades of remote mountain villages. Some also lay below us, lurking in the shadows of deep valleys.

One of the latter was Ripalimosani and we descended to

it. As Liz nosed her way over the cobbles of the main street, we were mobbed by a score of children, all of whom had a lean and hungry look. Fran ran up her window, expecting them, as she told me later, to begin unbolting the fenders and unscrewing the wheels. But I was not unduly worried.

On a September day in 1943 I had taken my jeep and gone searching for the most valuable commodity then to be had in Italy: fresh eggs. My quest took me towards the Biferno River, along whose far bank the Germans had established their winter defence line. A little village below me appeared peaceful enough; furthermore, I could hear cocks crowing, so down I went.

When the jeep clattered over the cobbles of the main street of Ripalimosani, all hell broke loose. Church bells began clanging like metallic fireworks. Children beyond counting emerged from the houses and swarmed aboard, until I was like to be smothered by a panting, screaming, ecstatic blanket of human flesh. It dawned on me that I was the first Allied soldier to "liberate" this village.

I was rescued by the mayor, an elderly gentleman who escorted me to the village hall where the townsfolk and I had a celebration. Many bottles of Asti Spumante were exploded; many speeches were made; and there was much back-slapping to be endured. The village band assembled and the brazen blat of badly played trumpets filled the air.

I asked meekly if anyone had any eggs, but this *non sequitur* was ignored. Another interruption did, however, catch everyone's attention. Alerted by the turmoil in Ripalimosani, the Germans across the river began shelling it. I fled the village faster than I had entered — *sans* eggs!

Paradiso

OUR original intention had been to travel south to the Straits of Messina then into Sicily but now we decided to abandon the battlefields itinerary and the far too vivid memories they evoked, and head for a place that had solaced me once before.

The great promontory of Monti Lattari juts out into the Tyrrhenian Sea between the gulfs of Napoli and Salerno. The Isle of Capri at its western tip has long been famous, as has Sorrento and the northern coast. The south coast was less well known. During the winter of 1944 a sympathetic senior officer gave me a week's leave from the hell's broth around Ravenna and I spent it in Positano, an ancient village of seafaring folk clinging to the great cliffs of the promontory's southern coast. If my stay there did not exactly heal me, it at least reassured me that life could still be worth living. So it was towards Positano that Fran and I now made our way.

Our descent from the central mountains was leisurely. Not that we had much choice. The roads had been so heavily damaged by military traffic that they were still under repair. Men, women, and children were working on roadside rock piles and the flat crack of hammers on stone made a kind of obbligato for our passage.

Once when we paused to drink wine by a mountain stream, a bevy of teenage girls sprang out of nowhere and subjected us to as minute an examination as if we had been insects and they entomologists. They were not solemn about it. One found some wet, brown moss that she plastered on her face in a fair imitation of my beard, and that sent them all off into gales of laughter. Then, as if to make amends, they vanished, only to return bearing handfuls of wild currants, which they gravely offered us.

It was a relief to reach Salerno, for the day's driving had exhausted me, but the worst was yet to come. The road along the south side of the Lattari promontory was little more than a narrow shelf chiselled into the almost-sheer face of the mountain, made more difficult by a succession of switchbacks and tunnels. Signs warned of falling rocks, but there were no warnings about the huge diesel buses that leapt out at us from tunnel mouths, hooting horribly, and hungrily grinding their gears.

It began to rain and the Tyrrhenian Sea began to smoke, fading from transparent sapphire to the blurry blue of kittens' eyes. Lemon and orange groves were everywhere in fruit. We crawled past a string of what, in medieval times, had been maritime city states; now shrunken to villages — Vietri, Maiori, Minori, Amalfi, Praiano, and, finally, Positano.

There are really only two directions in Positano — up, and down. Cemented to a nearly vertical slope, the stone buildings ascend upon one another's shoulders, giving the impression that the bottom house is carrying the whole on its back. Winding, often tortuous, flights of stone steps are the principal thoroughfares; donkeys, hand barrows, and occasional motor scooters, the chief means of transport. It was no place for the automobile. We could hardly find room in the small *piazza* beside the harbour to park Liz.

We asked a lean little man with a sardonic smile about Casa Bertolli, where I had stayed nine years earlier. He replied in English: "Ah, Casa Bertolli! Alas, it is no more. I think it slipped into the sea. But—" he grinned wolfishly "—I, Giuseppi Tommasino, am manager of Casa Maresca, where you and the lovely *signora*," he paused significantly, "will *not* fall into the sea."

Half an hour later we were sitting on the balcony of Casa Maresca eating crisply fried young chicken and drinking white Vesuvian wine, occasionally glancing at the sea far, far below.

Giuseppi hovered over us. Setting an espresso down before

me he asked, "The last time we met, *signore*, was in Amalfi, no?"

At the time of my earlier visit Amalfi had been a British officers' enclave from which we colonials were excluded. When a First Division artilleryman and I decided to put this snobbery to the test, we were thrown out of the Amalfi officers' club.

Giuseppi had been the club's barman on that occasion and, improbable as it may seem, remembered me from that one chance visit.

His was the kind of memory that makes me nervous. He had other remarkable attributes, including the ability to speak five languages, all learned on the promontory, beyond which he had never felt the urge to travel.

After lunch Giuseppi introduced us to the owner. A pre-war emigrant to the United States, rotund John Maresca had been a wholesale fruit dealer in New York for fifteen years, then had served in the U.S. army for five. By war's end he had saved enough to return to Positano and buy the ancestral villa, which he then turned into a most comfortable small hotel, each of whose ten rooms boasted a modern American bathroom.

Next morning Fran and I descended to the harbour, which crouched at the foot of soaring cliffs. Several fishing boats were drawn up on the small crescent of beach. They were rather similar to Newfoundland dories, hard-chined and double-ended. I made up my mind to go to sea in one if it could be arranged.

Positano's ambience seemed not entirely Italian. Its premier church, brooding over the harbour, looked more Greek Orthodox than Roman Catholic. A pair of terracotta black-amoors staring boldly at passers-by from the portico of a business house recalled distant days when merchant ships from Africa sailed into this harbour.

Sinuous alleyways and stairways spread all through the village. Wandering along them we came to a carpenter's workshop carved into the living rock. Two older and two young men (doubtless apprentices) were working in the shadowed gloom within. The young men were whipsawing planks by hand from a chestnut log, singing as they hauled the long saw back and forth between them.

Furniture appeared to be the chief product: heavy, durable stuff with deeply carved designs reminiscent of ancient Attic motifs. However, one of the older men was making intricate and delicate inlays in ebony jewellery boxes, using minute slivers of rare woods of variegated colours. Although I do not read Greek, I was sure I recognized Greek letters in the ornate designs.

The village's one policeman saluted us as he putted by on his motor scooter, his daughter clasped in front of him. According to Giuseppi, he had little to do. "There are no criminals here ... except people who come from Napoli and even they, if they stay long enough, become honest."

Everyone we met was courteous in the extreme; even the children, who carried themselves very straight, not out of pride, it seemed, but out of confidence. When they stopped beside us it was not to beg for cigarettes or candy, as sometimes happened elsewhere, it was to pass the time of day as if we were friends of their own age.

There were then only four other guests at Casa Maresca: an elderly English teacher; a pretty girl from the U.S. Embassy in Berlin; and George Sherwood, a BOAC pilot recently married to Shirley, a stewardess with the same airline. Giuseppi treated us all as members of the family, but some were treated more so than others. George told us about a pompous London solicitor who had just departed.

"Bit of an ass, really. Knew all about everything and didn't hesitate to say so. Giuseppi was serving liqueurs after dinner when this chappie announced to one and all that Italians made rotten soldiers. I thought he might get a liqueur down his neck, but Giuseppi just gave him that wicked smile and said, 'You know, *signore*, you are full of shit. That is nature, eh? But it is not nature for it to come out both ends.' The chappie left next morning."

In the manner of strangers abroad, we four quickly became comrades. One morning George and Shirley accompanied us down the 514 (Fran counted them) steps that led to a minute, rock-bound beach directly below Casa Maresca. My legs had turned to jelly by the time we reached the bottom.

A thunderhead eased its black bulk over the mountains as we swam, and torrential rain hissed bombastically into the sea around us. This turned out to be a short-lived respite from a blazing sun that drove us to seek the shade of a water-worn cave nearby.

It was already occupied by three fishermen snoozing on a pile of nets. Sleepily, they welcomed us. George had brought a bottle of wine, which the seven of us soon emptied. Then the fishermen, all youngish men, produced a bottle of *grappa*. It went the same way.

The climb back to Casa Maresca was an ordeal made somewhat more endurable by the stunning luxuriance of the plants and trees growing on narrow ledges painstakingly hewn from the face of the cliff. Fat lemons, bright oranges, and luscious kumquats hung everywhere.

From every rock and cranny, sly, sagacious little lizards eyed us and the flies — the flies with the most interest. The lizards were also to be found on the beaches where they were not above playing practical jokes such as scampering, tail held high, across the bellies of sunbathing maidens.

A new house was being built halfway up and I made this an excuse to rest in the shade of a kumquat tree. The workers were young, robust, deeply tanned, dressed in torn and tattered scraps of clothing. They whistled and sang fetchingly, especially while Shirley and Fran were within earshot.

An older man, doubtless the master builder, was observing a plumb line with the concentration of a pagan priest interrogating an oracle. Others were building a stone wall using mortar that appeared to consist of ordinary earth thickened with lime. It looked like the stuff of a child's mud pie and would have given a Canadian contractor palpitations.

Building stone quarried from cliffs overhanging another beach was brought up the stairway on men's backs. Most of the materials had to be brought to the site in this way, although donkeys were sometimes pressed into use.

The finished houses of ordinary folk were painted white inside and out, but on the high headlands stood some ornate villas resplendent in saffron, pink, and salmon. When I asked Giuseppi who owned these showy mansions he replied short-ly, "Money owns them. Dollars, pounds, marks, francs, and lira. Birds of paradise fly to them from all over the world, roost a while then fly away again. Some people here are happy to live on their excretions."

It became our custom to have a drink on the *portico* as we waited for the sudden dark to fall. After midnight, when Positano's electricity died, we would see a scatter of flicker-ing lights far out from the black loom of land. The fishermen were about their business. A few decades earlier they had fished by the light of torches soaked in pitch or oil. Now they used acetylene flares.

I had told Giuseppi I wanted to go fishing, and one moon-lit evening he reported that two fishermen were waiting on the beach below to take me out. I hurried down the stairs to find a boat nosed up on the sand and a pair of stalwart young men standing by. One identified himself as Pietro; the other as Giuseppi's brother-in-law, Ferdinando.

This would not be a normal working trip, they told me, because the moon, being almost full, made too much competition for our light. Nevertheless they lit the lamp suspended from an iron framework in the bow and we pushed off.

The acetylene hissed like a serpent and the tin reflector sent a beam of brilliant white light into the water, where it became a crepuscular glow, vaguely illuminating the sandy bottom two or three fathoms down.

Ferdinando rowed while Pietro stood poised in the bow with a long and slender trident in his hand. No fishes of any size were to be seen, but occasionally he made a graceful thrust at shadows under our keel, more for effect, I think, than with intent.

Night birds cried from the cliffs as we slid silently past little white beaches and the black mouths of grottoes. From time to time, a bottle of *grappa* passed between us. We shared a companionable silence. Suddenly a flying fish rose close to the boat and Pietro speared it on the wing. It lay in the scuppers, iridescent colours shimmering as it died.

Pietro speared a couple of crabs, then Ferdinando spotted an octopus. The spear flashed and a sepia cloud showed that the thrust had gone home. The creature was brought aboard, dangling limply and, I hoped, already dead because Ferdinando immediately tore it apart. He pulled out the white, rubbery siphon tubes and gave them to me. I knew I was being greatly honoured because the tubes are considered an uncommon delicacy. There being no help for it, I swallowed them with a sauce of sea water.

As the boat drifted on in its aura of spectral light, the young men began to talk about their trade. It did not seem either very demanding or very onerous. They fished close to land, mostly within the confines of their own bay; they usually fished only in fair weather on nights without a moon. There was no competition since only five boats had the right to fish Positano Bay — a number arrived at by consensus, not determined by law. Rather than compete with one another in the manner of Canadian fishermen, the crews of the five vessels co-operated. If one boat found a school the others would converge upon it, each with a broad dip net poised to slide under the light-bedazzled fishes. Sometimes one boat would set a purse seine while the others surrounded and herded the school. Group catches were shared between all the crews. When tuna appeared off the coast, boats from several villages might league together.

For the most part the fishes caught were small and, to my way of thinking, scarce. I was at a loss to see how a fisherman could make a living, and said so.

"We don't need so much," said Ferdinando. "We build our own boats and knit our own nets so they cost nothing. We take our catch to the market at dawn and sell it to the people who are going to eat it so there are no *banditos* between us and them to make a profit off both. When we go home to our families, we usually have enough lire to buy what is needed."

"If we wanted more money we'd have to catch more fish," Pietro interjected. "*Si*, and more and more, until we caught them all. Then what? Go to Napoli and get a job in a factory? No, *signore*, not me. Not even if I could buy a *cara* like yours. Me, I am happy enough to know there'll be some fish for Ferdinando and me to catch tomorrow and, by God's grace, the next day too."

To which Ferdinando added: "Dottore Magnani, who is of the university in Roma and comes to Positano in the winter, says our forefathers fished here before Christ was born. They must have taken only what they needed, or there would be nothing left, *si*? We try to do the same so our sons can do what we are doing."

It was after midnight when they landed me on the beach, together with a wicker basket containing the whole of our meagre catch, instructing me to tell Giuseppi to cook it. The moon was sinking and they were going back out onto the black mirror of the bay to fish seriously till dawn. As I toiled up the interminable steps, I wondered how long they and theirs would be able to go on living as they chose.

Positano was home to several notable outlanders. There was, for instance, a skeletal and deeply tanned Irishman with a black beard hanging to his bare navel that made him look like an Abyssinian Christ. He went everywhere tenderly holding hands with an enormously fat Italian mama. He told us he was a painter — when the mood was on him.

"It seldom is," he sighed, "because, you see, I am in the toils of the stars and can only work when Betelgeuse is in the ascendant."

There were other visitors from the Auld Sod. One evening the peace of the *piazza* was shattered by the arrival of a 1930s touring car bearing three wild-eyed, wild-haired Dubliners. They drove drunkenly around and around the little square, shrilling Gaelic challenges at the natives . . . who responded with benign smiles.

Then there was a beautiful swivel-hipped youth who went about barefoot in a sort of toga, carrying a bouquet of flowers. The scion of a famous American political family, he was part of a little colony of homosexuals living in a rose-pink villa high on the cliffs, drifting with the changing seasons from the Côte d'Azur to Rapallo then back to Positano.

Several villas in the neighbourhood were for sale and John Maresca showed us one. A labyrinth of intricate stonework on the shoulder of a cliff so steep that no two rooms were on the same level, it boasted a private beach and a grotto, together with an acre of pomegranates, oranges, and bougainvillaeas. The price was fifty thousand dollars Canadian. I decided I would have to write a best seller one of these days.

We made friends with the owner of a grocery store where, along with local men, Fran and I would perch on huge jars of olive oil, nibbling olives stuffed with anchovies and drinking dry white wine. Fran's presence did not seem to inhibit the conversation, though I suspect it was cleaned up somewhat in deference to her.

The chief topic was the forthcoming national election. Communist and Socialist supporters were evidently in the majority locally but everyone seemed united against resurgent Fascism, as represented by the local candidate for the Christian Democratic Party, who had collaborated with the Germans.

Positano did not take its politics as seriously as did the city of Sorrento. One day we drove Giuseppi there and while he went about some errands we set out to see the town. This was not easily done. As with Coronation London, Sorrento was largely concealed from view by posters. All available wall space having been consumed, election posters had been pasted on the sidewalks and even on the streets.

They were colourful. Red stars and hammers and sickles made brilliant splashes. The Royalists favoured royal blue, while the Fascists were relatively sedate in black and white. The mammoth posters of the Christian Democrats were rainbow-hued, as if to outshine all the others. The whole kaleidoscopic assemblage was in constant flux as party workers vigorously papered over their opponents' posters.

Because it was the thing for tourists to do, Giuseppi insisted we drive on to Pompeii. This was a mistake. The ruins were jammed with tourists, guides, and shills — a far cry from the way things had been when I visited Pompeii in 1944. Then there had been only a sprinkling of service men and women. A Canadian nurse and I stocked one of the resurrected little wine shops with *vino* from supplies stashed in my jeep, and dispensed it freely to all comers. The ghosts of the buried town had seemed to walk again that day.

Nothing so evocative occurred on my second visit. Back at Casa Maresca, I lamented that it was not any more possible to recapture the taste and texture of Pompeiian times.

"You wanna know how people lived way back then?" John Maresca asked. "I guess *I* could show you how *some* of 'em made out, only we gotta go pretty near to Vietri, if you don' mind the drive."

Potters in the Caves

NEXT morning we three headed eastward along the serpentine road by which Fran and I had reached Positano. I drove very slowly in order to see something of the scenery. John played the guide, telling us about the spectacular little villages along the way.

One was particularly striking. It could not be seen from the road unless one stopped and hung over the balustrade to look almost straight down several hundred feet. A collection of stone huts huddled near a tiny beach at the landward end of a narrow crevice. The sea boiled and raged in the narrow entrance, preventing boats from passing in or out except when the tide was high.

It was, in effect, a roofless cavern into which the sun struck for only an hour or two each day. To reach it by land demanded an hour's descent down precipitous slopes. John explained that until the 1920s a large and prosperous village had existed here, but an earthquake and tidal wave had sent the sea lunging so far up the gully that when it retreated nothing remained. The place was now generally shunned.

All the villages on this coast had suffered major earthquakes. In the eleventh century, Amalfi had had as many as fifty thousand inhabitants, and stood as high as the Venetian republic in Mediterranean affairs, until earthquakes and tidal waves brought it down.

Until the end of the nineteenth century, when the road was built, the towns had evolved largely independent of one another. Even now the people of Amalfi are physically different from others on the coast, with darker colouring and a distinctly Moorish cast to their features.

The differences are not limited to appearances. Thus Minori is a disreputable, raffish village with a Neapolitan ebullience, whereas Maiori, only a few miles distant, is rigorously neat but filled with suspicious peasantry, hostile not only to strangers but even to neighbouring communities as well.

As we neared the eastern end of Monti Lattari, John directed us off the highway down a dirt track to the sea. The track then doubled back to the westward along a narrow strip of beach at the base of monumental cliffs that were honeycombed by wave-cut caverns.

Inhabited by paleolithic people at least fifty thousand years ago, these caves have continued to shelter human beings ever since. In our time a jumbled warren of brick and stone structures blended into the rock walls, masking the entrance to many of the caves.

John motioned me to stop before one particularly haphazard-looking construct. Plastered against the cliffs to a height of three and four storeys, it looked to be in panic-stricken retreat from an encroaching sea. A small and faded sign hanging askew below a window proclaimed that this was the *Ceramica Artistica Solimene.*

"Now," said John, getting out of the car, "I gonna show you how life she was like in Pompeii, and maybe long before."

We entered a narrow yard crowded with bundles of faggots, and by two shallow, rectangular ponds filled with grey muck that glistened in the bright sunlight. John led us through a low door into a maze of passageways redolent of charcoal smoke, cooking, and other domestic odours. Children scurried about, and several robust, good-looking women nodded politely from inner doorways. This many-tiered labyrinth seemed little more than a rather dilapidated tenement . . . until we met Marco Solimene.

Marco was sitting at his kitchen table when John ushered us in and introduced us. He was a big man, still powerful looking despite thinning grey hair. Courteous to a fault, he bowed to Fran before pouring each of us a cool cup of wine from a sweat-beaded earthenware jug. He seemed delighted when John told him we wanted to see the *ceramica*.

"Indeed! Indeed! Then you *will* see it . . . everything we have . . . but first you must meet Papa."

Papa was Vincenzo Solimene, a strongly featured man who had spent the bulk of his eighty years at a potter's wheel, barefooted in winter mists or summer's heat. When we met him he was old and ill but still the unchallenged patriarch.

He and his four middle-aged sons were the master potters in a work force numbering over forty men, women, and children. All lived together as one familial community in a maze of rooms and passages where workshops and living quarters, caves and external constructs, were inextricably combined.

Work began as play. Infants of both sexes puddled clay in the courtyard while older children modelled crude figurines or made toy cups, plates, and pots. Boys began practising the true potter's trade in their early teens. When a wheel became idle, one of them would slip behind it to shape a little vase or jug, throwing it back into the clay pile when completed.

According to Marco, not more than three or four boys or men had left the *ceramica* during his lifetime to try their hand at other work; and two of these had since returned.

"We don't like being apart," Marco explained. "We feel good when we all work here together."

The Solimenes constituted an almost self-sufficient tribe within which most things were shared. Money was of little account. Food, wine, and such essential "store goods" as could not be made at home were obtained by barter. Most other requirements were to be had from the land or from the sea at no cost. I could understand why one would be loath to leave.

All pottery begins as clay, called *terra* by Italian potters. The best *terra*, Marco told me, was that which had been laid down by swift-flowing rivers. River clay tends to be of uniform consistency, with the worst of the impurities washed out of it. The Solimenes got their *terra* from riverine deposits a few miles beyond Vietri and brought it back to the pottery in two-wheeled wooden carts drawn by donkeys.

Modern potteries rely on complicated grinding and clarifying machinery to prepare the clay but the Solimenes needed no such aids. I watched two scantily clad young men dragging wicker baskets filled with raw *terra* to a stone floor in the open courtyard where they pulverized the lumps with mighty wooden mallets. They then shovelled the crushed clay into one of the rectangular stone basins we had noticed on our arrival. Water was added and the mixture stirred with wooden rakes until it became a soupy slurry which was then bucketed into the second pond, leaving behind a layer of rock fragments and other detritus.

Surplus water was evaporated by the sun's heat until all

that remained was a thick layer of grey slime, which was spread to dry on the stones of the courtyard, again pulverized, then stored as powder till needed by the potters.

A call came for more *terra* as Marco and I were standing by the storage bins. A long-faced, toothy little gamin immediately began filling and carrying pails of the purified dust to an enormous stone mixing bowl. Under Marco's watchful eye, the boy added a measured quantity of water then jumped into the bowl. His splayed feet squelched and slushed about, mixing the clay to the desired plasticity. This looked like fun, and as the soft muck spurted up between his toes the boy smiled in perfect bliss. Marco had to pretend to threaten him with a wooden rake to make him desist.

Now an older boy shovelled up a basketful of the mix and carried it off. We followed as he trotted buoyantly beneath a fifty-pound load over slippery stones and sodden boardwalks to an arched masonry wall flush with the cliff. The doorway was small and set at such an angle we had to lean a bit to enter the cave that stretched dimly beyond. Distorted shafts of sunlight from openings far above quickly dissipated, but kerosene lamps hanging on the grotto walls gave enough light to see by. The residue from centuries of potting lay thickly everywhere. An odour of mildew filled the damp air and moulds and fungi grew on the walls and on the clay-coated floor.

Four slime-coated wooden potters' wheels dominating the cavern were almost indistinguishable from those depicted in paintings from early Pharaonic times. Each consisted of a plank bench on which the potter rested his buttocks while, with one bare foot, he spun a heavy counterweight wheel set at floor level. A vertical shaft squeaked against wet wood as it spun a smaller second wheel at chest level. On this erratically revolving platform the potter's lean fingers shaped the clay.

A water pot, sunk to its lips in slime and sporting a growth of delicate yellow fungi, stood beside each wheel so the potters could moisten their fingers from time to time.

The potters stopped their wheels when we appeared. Not until we had been introduced and offered a cup of wine did they return to work. Then it was as if we no longer existed. Each man's attention seemed entirely concentrated on the lump of *terra* before him. A vase rose wraith-like from one wheel. Spinning in the gloom, its wet flanks swelled and shrank as if performing a sensuous dance.

I had seen potters at work before — in bright, modern studios using power-driven wheels embodying many elements of modern science. I had been impressed. In the Solimenes' cave I was mesmerized. This was no mere imitation of antiquity I was beholding. The card castle of time collapsed and I was transported into an earlier world.

The four potters dwelt in that world. When Marco told us they often worked ten- or even twelve-hour days, I was astonished and muttered something about slave labour. John overheard me.

"No," he said firmly. "They don' work so hard because they gotta. They work because they like-a what they do! *Ceramica artistica* is in the blood!"

It must have been so. Marco told us that Solimenes had been spinning potters' wheels for at least ten generations. Whether or not they loved their work, unquestionably they were wedded to it.

We left the cave and went to see the kiln. It was an amazing structure. In some far-distant time three rooms of a triple-tiered house plastered against the cliff had been converted to a new purpose. Wooden floors and ceilings had been removed and replaced with clay gratings, and the walls had been thickened with extra bricks.

The lower room was now the furnace. Since wood was scarce and costly, the fire was fed mostly with faggots made of small branches, dead grape vines, and bracken bound tightly into bundles. These burned fiercely, but were consumed so quickly the fire had to be fed every ten or twenty minutes.

Heated air and smoke rose through clay grates into the second room, then into the upper one to escape finally through a yawning hole in the roof.

Most pottery was fired for from two to three days. While firing was in progress youths and boys, streaming with sweat, trotted between the faggot piles and the furnace by day and by night. Plebian pottery emerged rough textured and reddish-brown in colour. Wine amphorae of the ancient world had been made just so, and the Solimenes actually made amphorae for hill men of the Potenza region who would store their wine in no other kind of container.

In a room high up on the cliff face, we found two of Marco's uncles and two apprentices sitting around a wooden table discoloured by centuries of spilt pigments. One of the uncles was decorating a teapot with a complicated arrangement of sea anemones, squids, and dolphins.

The other uncle — a small, dark man — was making a massive bas-relief wall plaque, twelve feet long and six high. The scene, a mountain vista sloping to the sea, was populated by donkeys, goats, and shepherd boys and girls disporting themselves amongst olive trees and cacti.

We were told the plaque would be cut into a number of pieces for firing, after which it would be reassembled on the wall of a fishermen's café in Minori.

At noon a handsome girl came into the painters' room and called us for dinner. We ate in Marco's home — three rooms in the middle tier of the crazy pile. His wife and three daughters served us tomato-and-eggplant soup, followed by *maccheroni alla marinara*, which seemed appropriate since marine motifs dominated the Solimene pottery.

As we were finishing, old Vincenzo was helped into the room by another of his potter sons. Everyone stood up, but he waved us back to our benches. He had come, he said in a voice resonating with authority, to apologize for the inadequacy of our reception. Had John only warned him in advance — here he fixed John with an accusing glare — we would have eaten roast kid and other good things fitting for visitors from across the seas.

I protested, but he would have none of that and, with a smile for Fran and another glare at John, departed leaving Marco subdued and his wife almost in tears. There was no question as to who was chief of the Solimene clan.

After lunch Marco led us into yet another cave, even darker than the first. It was dominated by a lowering structure that could have been mistaken for a medieval torture machine. A massive columnar section of tree trunk rose from a circular stone pedestal some ten feet in diameter. Four crude wooden arms projected from the column at about half its height. From each dangled lengths of heavy chain attached at their lower ends to slabs of rock the size and shape of grave markers. These lay horizontally on the pedestal base. The whole structure was so thickly coated in rock dust as to appear fossilized.

This, Marco explained, was where the Solimenes ground the silica sands to make their glazes, and the natural oxides to make their pigments.

"Don't they buy *anything*?" I asked John in an aside.

He grinned. "Nothin' much. . . well, maybe some matches to light the fires . . . if they don't still use flint and steel."

The grinding mill was powered by a donkey harnessed to

a fifteen-foot horizontal shaft keyed into the central column. We watched as Marco shovelled glittering white sand onto the pedestal then slapped the donkey into reluctant activity. Round and round the little beast plodded while the arms of the device towed the grinding stones over the spread sand. The clanking chains and rasping stones made an infernal noise, and a rising pall of dust began to fill the air. We were glad to stumble out of the cave into sunshine again.

I felt sorry for the donkey; but John told me it had to do this kind of work only an hour or two every few days and, for the rest, lived a normal donkey's life . . . whatever that may have been.

When we said our goodbyes to the Solimenes late that afternoon, I did so with no little envy. If there is any such thing as a sense of place and certainty to be had in our world it seemed to me the Solimenes had it. But then, of course, they did not really live in our world.

Arrivederci Italia

DURING the remainder of our stay in Positano we strolled and lolled. The cumulonimbus cloud that lived in the mountains behind us sailed over regularly each afternoon and spewed out rain enough to set the gulleys roaring and bring uncountable numbers of small snails out of niches and cracks in the masonry to silver the rocks with their mucous trails.

One morning Fran and I borrowed a small skiff rejoicing in the name of *Elene*. With much sweat and some blistering, I rowed for several miles under the headlands. There was a long swell running that foiled our efforts to beach on tempting patches of sand half-hidden between black basaltic rocks.

We passed a cave mouth the size of a cathedral some hundreds of feet above the sea. A small white *casa* stood in the opening like a single tooth in a monster gape. There seemed no apparent way of reaching the place by land or sea. Perhaps it was the home of a troglodyte. There *was* one such in Positano, living in a tiny house perched on a crag, requiring an hour's climb up a goat track to reach it. I do not know what his philosophy was but it must have been exalted.

The sad day came when we had to make our farewells. Giuseppi suggested we delay our departure until the morrow but we ignored his advice, waved goodbye, and drove northward past cloud-veiled Vesuvio. Beyond Napoli we turned inland. By then we knew why Giuseppi had urged a postponement. Today was the feast of Corpus Christi and every town and village in Italy was clogged with religious pageantry.

Not even the highways were exempt. A vast, lugubrious, and attenuated procession on the open road beyond Capua slowed us to a crawl. The men appeared bored and out of sorts as they tramped down the centre of the pavement, each carrying a dingy flag representing some holy personage. The women were ecstatic, not to say possessed. Ragged groups of children under the nominal control of black-robed priests, some mouthing songs of praise. Some chose opportune moments to pitch stones at the wheels of the Hillman as we slunk by.

Now we swung north towards the Liri Valley and Cassino. Low volcanic hills, hard and desolate, swelled around us, looking so much like parts of north Africa that I almost expected

Bedouins on camels to come cantering into view. For the first time since leaving the Campobasso country, we again began to see ruins that spoke of recent war.

Dun-coloured skies hung over the valley as we approached the mile-long, arrow-straight stretch of road leading into Cassino town. In 1944 it had been known as the Mad Mile, and many men had met death upon it.

The old town had been all but obliterated. Indeed, considering the cataract of destruction poured down upon it for almost half a year, it was surprising that anything man-made remained. With the possible exception of Stalingrad, no other victim of the war had been subjected to the destructive forces of "conventional" warfare unleashed upon Cassino. An estimated twenty to thirty thousand tons of shells, together with at least ten thousand tons of aerial bombs, fell upon the town and the Benedictine monastery on its overlooking peak.

We drove up the switchback road expecting to find the monastery also in ruins, but it had been meticulously restored. It was difficult to understand why such an enormous expenditure of time, money, and materials had been committed to the rebuilding of this huge square block of a structure, which was about as architecturally stimulating as a prison.

The freshly paved parking lot was filled with Mercedes-Benz buses and Volkswagens; the whole place swarmed with German tourists bedecked with cameras and binoculars.

My cold gorge rose as I recalled how, soon after the war

ended, our political and business leaders hastened to Germany's aid. I remembered how the U.S. Marshall Plan alone had contributed billions of dollars' worth of equipment and materials to the resuscitation of our recent, deadly enemy, while at the same time many of the countries that had been savaged and ravaged by the Nazis, but were not considered politically acceptable, continued to endure the direst of post-war privations.

The contents of the parking lot before me was powerful evidence of the success of our rescue operations. With our help, Germany had risen from the ashes of the Third Reich just as it had done from the ashes of Kaiser Wilhelm's empire. It was a resurrection I could not contemplate with equanimity.

Fran would have liked to tour the monastery but I could not stomach the presence of all those complacent *Herrenvolk* gawking across the plains below us where so many thousands of soldiers, friends of mine amongst them, had perished.

"We're going on to Rome," I said. "Right now!"

So we dropped down into the valley and drove north at speed between the two mountain ranges that contain the Liri. Although brief and violent storms showered us with rain and hail, I did not even stop to put up Liz's canvas top, but drove on as if pursued by devils.

The only affordable place we could find in Rome was a rather shabby hostel frequented by Italian commercial travellers. A working man's café stood nearby so we went in for a vermouth. Politically aroused men and women almost filled the place, shouting and screaming at one another. This was bedlam, so we fled to the streets.

It was still Corpus Christi day, and Rome was still the capital of Catholic Christendom. Half the city seemed to be marching; the other half watching. We tried to avoid the mobs but each detour brought us up against another sweating mass of humanity. Fran wanted to visit the Colosseum, now encrusted with rows of bellowing loudspeakers, but thousands of Romans were jamming the portals, intent on seeing a display of religious floats inside the ancient walls. Had one of the old emperors been staging a contest between Christians and lions, I *might* have been willing to brave the mob. Not otherwise.

Rome was awash in political propaganda. Every available inch of wall space was plastered with posters and their tone was much more violent than those we had so far seen. Nothing was barred. Vicious Communist posters faced equally savage Fascist ones, with unctuous Democratic Christian propaganda sandwiched in between. Here were none of the sometimes humorous ripostes we had seen on the Adriatic Coast and in the south. This was deadly stuff. Not even the clergy were immune. I watched two friars pause before a papier mâché figure of Lenin and, after a surreptitious glance around, spit on it. Not far away a Communist street-corner orator routed a small group of clergy by describing their parentage in barnyard language.

We rose early next day feeling compelled to see some sights. We went first to St. Peter's where we admired the Piazza but were less impressed by the Basilica, which has to be the earth's outstanding example of unbridled ostentation.

Inside I showed Fran a discovery I had made during a visit in 1944 — a small naked cherub so exquisitely sculptured that generations of visitors had been unable to resist the impulse to pat his bare backside, which was worn smooth and somewhat sunken as a result of too much admiration.

We paid our shot and went into the treasury where a world's ransom was displayed for the glory of God. Most of the jewelled and golden articles had merit only in their financial worth. Some pieces, notably by Cellini, were indeed lovely but the majority were gaudy gewgaws overblown with precious stones and metals.

As we made our way out, we did not fail to notice the brass inlays in the floor of the Basilica intended to impress on visitors just how much larger St. Peter's is than any other Christian church.

We drove along the Tiber to the Ostia Gates and stopped at St. Paul's Without the Walls. The nave was almost in darkness and rows of unadorned pillars stretched away to cool and distant recesses. One could decently worship one's gods in the dim cloisters of this church.

By then it was nearly noon so we decided to be away. Scudding bursts of rain lashed the car as we drove across the Plains of Campania into the rolling hills of Tuscany and on to Siena to spend the night.

Our hotel room overlooked a mad jumble of roofs, towers, and spires. At a quarter to six the famous bells began to sound, the smaller ones hastening time in order to be heard before the giants spoke. I could count the swinging bronze of fifteen sets. The vibrations struck against wheeling clouds of chimney swifts, dispersing them as if they were no more than flights of midges.

Next morning we drove on through a prosperous landscape with fine, brick-built farms straddling the ridges, each with its attendant stand of soaring cypresses. We lunched at a roadside inn beside the Arno, within sight of the towers of Florence.

When the regiment came here in August of 1944, the Germans still held the north bank of the river and our troops the south. Although Florence had been declared an open city, the Germans reminded us that they were not to be trifled with by firing occasional artillery salvos.

One afternoon I had gone looking for a place to establish an observation post from which our artillery could direct counter-battery fire. I came upon a riverside estate behind whose high walls rose the cupola of a small *palazzo*. Thinking it might serve the purpose, I walked through the open gates. Attached to the *palazzo*, which was shabby and much neglected, was a large greenhouse. I peered in and saw it housed a sculptor's studio.

At that moment an 88mm shell screamed fiercely overhead and crashed into a row of houses beyond the walls of the estate. It sounded like a ranging shot, in which case a greenhouse would be a poor place near which to linger. I was about to dash for the shelter of the *palazzo* when movement behind the glass caught my eye. A white-haired man, handsome and erect, was working at what appeared to be a plaster bust. Another shell exploded and I dropped on my belly. When I cautiously rose again, the sculptor was still at work, apparently unperturbed.

Curiosity overmastering my respect for German artillery, I found a door and entered. The sculptor, who appeared to be in his seventies, glanced up. Laying down his tools, he came towards me, holding out both hands.

"Welcome, sir." The vibrant timbre of his voice belied his age. "Will you have some wine with me?"

As we sat on ornate iron chairs under that precarious roof, drinking his wine, I saw that the greenhouse studio was full of plaster casts and draped figures, but I could see no finished pieces.

"You observe that all my work is only clay and plaster," he said, smiling.

When I nodded in some embarrassment, he chuckled. "And you are curious? Then allow me to explain.

"You who are a soldier can perhaps understand what my friends in this city do not. They think me mad because I do not choose to quarrel with the years. Most men's lives are a struggle against time, a struggle to outwit it, to confound its passage. I have concluded that to spend one's life trying to outwit time is to play the fool, and I am no fool."

He paused to refill our glasses.

"You think this a strange way for a sculptor to speak? Perhaps it is. But man, who is himself as impermanent as eddies in a stream, can create nothing permanent.

"For many years I had my figures cast in bronze; then when I came to understand the futility of that I had them melted down. How long could they have outlasted me? A millennium or two, or three perhaps? A moment in the inexorable passage of the years. Now I work only in clay and plaster — materials of the moment — and harbour no more illusions of immortality."

I walked with him under that thin glass roof, which was surely symbolic of the way he looked at life. Fragile, impermanent, sufficient only to shelter him for the nonce. I am no judge of sculpture but I was awed by some of his work. His busts and figures had a serenity that seemed quite out of place in the world in which we were living.

There was a clay bust of a girl, almost life-size, not yet finished. He drew off the wet drapes that covered her and she was lovely. Knowing that in a few weeks her clay would dry, crack, and disintegrate, I was half-inclined to agree with the old man's friends and think him mad.

Two days later the Germans took note of the high cupola of the *palazzo* and presumably concluded, as I had done, that it could serve as an observation post. Their guns removed it with Teutonic thoroughness — together with most of the *palazzo*. The greenhouse went too. Perhaps the old sculptor escaped. I never knew. That night we moved out to take part in another battle on the Adriatic Coast.

———————————

Fran and I followed the wide, placid Arno River from Florence to Pisa, where we joined a new *autostrada* heading north along the coast. We soon found ourselves swamped in a torrent of motorcycles, cars, and buses so we abandoned the *autostrada* in favour of a secondary road that clung to the low and sandy coast.

For the rest of the way to La Spezia, a distance of about thirty miles, we were hemmed in on both sides by nearly continuous rows of bathing huts, cottages, beach cabins, hotels, and *pensiones*, the summer haunts of industrial workers from the Po Valley. However, since the season had not yet begun, we encountered almost no traffic. The drive had an eerie quality, as if we were passing through an endless ghost town.

La Spezia seemed tense and uneasy. Few people were on the streets, but squads of steel-helmeted riot police could be glimpsed practising street fighting in byways away from the main road. Considering that the morrow was election day and that La Spezia was a shipbuilding and industrial city with very little work for its people, Premier De Gasperi's government may have had reason to anticipate trouble.

Not liking the look of things, I headed west. By the time we reached Rapallo, sometimes touted as the Nice of Italy, it was dusk. The smell of foreign money hung over the place like a miasma and, although I had no doubt that Rapallians considered it the sweetest smell in all the world, we did not. A glance at the map showed us what appeared to be a little fishing village at the tip of a peninsula a few miles beyond Rapallo. We expected it would be more to our liking.

Portofino, the "little fishing village," turned out to be the Mecca of an international élite. Instead of fishing boats, the little harbour was crowded with yachts, some as large as small liners. The twisting, picturesque streets were encrusted with boutiques and filled with glittering automobiles and semi-naked, glistening millionaires of several sexes.

What were we to do? It was almost dark and we were tired. Refusing to be intimidated, we registered at the only visible hotel, the Albergo Splendido, which turned out to be splendid indeed. We shared it that night with Clark Gable, the Crown Prince of Sweden, some of the Aga Khan's family, and others such.

Portofino would have been a great place to wait out the election. Not a poster was to be seen, nor did we hear a word spoken about it. Portofino was far above such mundane affairs.

If we heard nothing about the election, we *did* hear that

Sir Edmund Hillary had scaled Everest. This news set us thinking about mountains — and changed our plans. We had intended to make our way back to England by the most direct route, but now: "What do you say we go over the Great St. Bernard Pass into Switzerland?" I asked my wife. "We'd at least get a look at Mont Blanc, and maybe the Matterhorn."

"*And* meet the St. Bernard dogs. Let's do it!"

A two-day-old copy of the *Times* was brought to us with our breakfast and in it Fran came across the news that the Little St. Bernard Pass had been snowbound and closed for a week. This was disconcerting since the Great St. Bernard is much higher — in fact, the highest pass in Europe. Nobody in Portofino seemed to know or care about travel conditions in the Alps, so we headed for Genoa and a tourist information service.

This being the morning of election day, I expected all hell would be busting loose in towns and villages along the way, but hardly a soul was stirring. There were no election mobs, no line-ups at the polls — in fact, we saw no sign of polls. Even church-goers seemed to be staying home. I thought I sensed something ominous about this inactivity after the weeks of hectic build-up.

A wild and twisting drive took us into Genoa where, after much searching, we located the tourist bureau. The unshaven, bleary-eyed youth on duty shook his head when we explained that we hoped to cross the Great St. Bernard. No one knew if that was possible, he told us. The telephone lines to the pass were down and not even the bureau at Aosta, at the foot of the pass, seemed to know what conditions were like up in the crags. He apologized for the lack of information, and then for his own hang-dog appearance. He was suffering from the election fever, which, properly fuelled, had kept most Italians up so late the previous night that few would appear again before noon. So much for my apprehensions.

We were in some doubt as to whether to proceed into the mountains. If both St. Bernard passes were closed, we might be marooned for days. We looked at one another.

"*I* think," said Fran, "we should press on . . . those dogs, you know."

So we turned north on the *autostrada* and crossed the Ligurian Apennines under a shroud of rain. Having put this first mountain barrier behind us and with the Pavia plains ahead, we abandoned the new highway.

The rain grew heavier and soon we were driving through an inundated world. Rice paddies stretched to the dull horizon on either side. The roads became dykes along whose wet and slippery backs Liz slithered. This country of *Bitter Rice* seemed unrelentingly dismal. We saw no one in the tiny villages except small patrols of saturated and miserable soldiers standing by to prevent rioting, which could not possibly have occurred unless the dead had risen from their graves. This was the quietest Sunday we had seen in Italy — as well as the wettest.

As we entered the mouth of the Aosta Valley we began catching glimpses of mountains through rifts in the overcast. The clouds became luminous with unseen sunlight. Slabs of wet, green stone in marble quarries along the road glowed eerily. Terraces stepped up steep slopes until they were lost in the high mists. They seemed to bear rank upon rank of squat temples, an illusion produced by the rows of stone pillars supporting grape trellises.

We climbed higher and the valley began to narrow. After a couple of hours it unexpectedly widened, revealing the city of Aosta. Here the road forked, one branch turning left towards the Little St. Bernard and France, the other disappearing to the right into a knife-slit in the mountain walls on its way to the Great St. Bernard and Switzerland.

It was almost dark and time for us to roost. The Albergo della Corone e Poste in Aosta's main square looked like our kind of place. Its several ancient buildings rambled around a roughly cobbled inner courtyard where post carriages had once rattled and horses been stabled. The rooms within were panelled in dark woods and dimly lighted by leaded windows.

All was presided over by three brothers in their sixties. The courtly middle brother, Frédéric, showed us where to sign the book. Balding, vivacious Domenico led us to our wainscotted room overlooking the square, then went out into the rain to stable Liz. Portly and rubicund François, the oldest brother, escorted us in to dinner then became our waiter, wine steward, and general factotum.

He served us minestrone, steamed trout, tender little steaks with artichokes, strawberries and cream, fresh apricots and cherries, cheeses, and a variety of local wines. Between times he entertained us with tidbits about the history of the Valle d'Aosta. We were the only guests, so the other brothers joined us for coffee and liqueurs.

Glowing with good food, wine, and company, we went to bed under a feather comforter. The steady rumble of pelting rain on lead-sheathed roofs sounded like a benison.

The rain pelted down all night, the wind whined in the chimney pots, and the barometer plummeted. After a late, luxurious breakfast I dashed across the square to the regional tourist office. The woman behind the desk shook her head regretfully.

"The St. Bernard passes are still closed, I think, *signore*; but if the telephone is working I will call."

It was a hand-cranked machine and for a long time produced no response. When it did, the news was not good. Two circular ploughs, one working from each direction, had failed to cut paths through the snow fields of the Great St. Bernard. A hurricane was blowing through the Little St. Bernard. Snow and sleet were beating down on both. . . .

She smiled sympathetically and slid some tourist pamphlets across the counter, suggesting we forget about the mountains for a week.

The Albergo Corone was warm and snug so we settled down for the day. Which turned out to be several days. During breaks in the weather, we walked about the old town or explored the countryside by car. For much of the time we sat in the snug drawing room of the hotel while one or other of the brothers regaled us with stories about the Valle.

The brothers were a saga unto themselves. Fleeing religious persecution, their paternal ancestor had come over the Little St. Bernard from France in the late sixteenth century.

"He was a dissenter from the Roman faith who only escaped burning because he had a good horse and good sense," François told us. "He led that horse, or it led him, across the pass in mid-winter. The Valle applauded independent ways so it took them in, horse and man. They went to work for a hostelry. Both had big families. In time our family took over this hotel, while the progeny of our ancestor's horse carried the mail and hauled coaches from one end of the Valle to the other."

"Yes," added Domenico, "and the offspring of both were all dissenters. They still are." He grinned at his brothers. "We manage not to agree on anything for very long."

There were no post horses at the hotel now, of course. The automobile had driven them out long since, but the equine branch of the family lived on in the nearby Gran Paradiso National Park, where they earned their living carrying visitors into an alpine wilderness.

The peaks and valleys of the Gran Paradiso were home to some of the last wild wolves in Europe, to the almost equally rare chamois (a sheep-like antelope), and to the ibex, the wild goat of Europe that, a century ago, was abundant all through the Alps but now survived, precariously, only in a few parks.

"All the wild creatures will go," said Frédéric gloomily. "That is man's law. Unless a creature lives with us as our slave it must go. Even the lammergeyer, that wonder of the skies, must go. That is man's law."

Lammergeyers are enormous birds of prey closely related to eagles. They existed in Europe only in the Gran Paradiso, where there were fewer than ten of them. Even in the park they were persecuted — for their eggs, which sold to rich collectors for as much as five thousand dollars each.

Election evening was devoted to heated discussions of the results. Frédéric was disgusted at how well the Communists had done and was not to be solaced by the fact that De Gasperi's Christian Democrats had retained power.

"Ninety percent of the Reds went out to vote despite this terrible weather," he fumed, "but less than a quarter of the Democrats. That is those devils' strength. *They* act!"

Adhering to the tradition of dissent, each brother had voted for a different party. François had supported the Socialists, and Domenico the Royalists. It was easy to be a political dissident in Aosta. In addition to the nine national parties, the citizens of the Valle had added four more of their own.

As far as most of its inhabitants were concerned, their valley was an independent state. I had thought I knew all the little states of Europe, but here was one I had never heard about. The brothers were happy to fill me in.

Valle d'Aosta is a titanic hand thrust into the heart of the Alps. Its northward-pointing fingers are the valleys down which flow the mountain streams that swell the Dora Baltea. One finger reaches into the glacial fields of Monte Rosa; a second into those of the Matterhorn; a third to the col of Great St. Bernard; and the fourth to Mont Blanc, the highest peak in Europe. The thumb points back southwest to the Little St. Bernard Pass. Frédéric, the historian of the family, showed us his collection of hand axes, projectile points, scrapers, and other stone tools, most of them from sites on the valley floor but some from the highest cols.

"People were crossing the Alps between glaciations as early as 250,000 years ago," he told us. "They came across both St. Bernard passes. Many must surely have perished in those snow-swept places. Can you imagine Neanderthals plodding through the blizzards up there? There were mammoths in this valley then. We sometimes find their tusks."

"What about modern man?" I asked.

"Ten thousand years ago the high valleys were home to the first shepherds — the first farmers, you might call them.

In winter they drove their half-wild flocks down to the lowlands. In summer they followed them up to the high alpine meadows, as our herdsmen do today.

"Much later, Celtic tribes came over the passes from the north. They held the Valle against all newcomers until 218 B.C. when Hannibal came out of Africa en route to Italy with fifty thousand foot soldiers, nine thousand cavalrymen, and thirty-seven elephants. The Celts blocked his path but he fought his way through them to the Little St. Bernard and, after incredible exertions, descended into our Valle. By then he had lost *all* his cavalry, *half* his foot soldiers, and all but a handful of elephants. What he and his men had to endure so impressed the ancient world that no other invaders tried to force the passes until two centuries later, when Julius Caesar sent his legions to seize them."

The Romans remained nearly four centuries. When their empire collapsed, the Valle again became its own country under tribal leaders, who built enormous stone forts along the main valley and its tributaries. In 1800 Napoleon brought an army south over the Great St. Bernard Pass to attack the Austrians in northern Italy and nearly missed the Battle of Marengo because of stubborn opposition from one of these ancient forts.

During the latter part of the nineteenth century, the kingdom of Italy tried to swallow the Valle. As Frédéric explained, it proved indigestible.

"We were one people, yet many people. In some valleys they still speak Swiss–German; others speak French; some speak Piedmontese; and there are traces of the tongues of the ancient races, the Celts, and even the shepherd folk. Yet we are one because we all dream of our own transalpine world where we can be our own masters."

Until the capitulation of Italy late in 1943, they were still nurturing their dream. Then tanks, guns, and trucks filled with *Wehrmacht* soldiers rolled into the valley. The Germans were not expecting more than token resistance. What they got was ferocious guerrilla warfare.

"You would not think it to look at us now — three old men getting fat — but we were all in the fight. Domenico spent the winter in the wild Tersiva mountains looking after the pack horses of the guerrilla army. Me, I stayed in town to organize the passage of messages, supplies, and arms. François was with a brigade laired near *le Petit-Saint-Bernard*. They closed the pass to the Germans so many times the *tedeschi* gave up and it stayed closed."

Although the Germans inflicted terrible reprisals on the people of the Valle, they could never mass sufficient troops to crush the resistance. Some months before the end of the war they were forced to withdraw. The Valle had been liberated through the efforts of its own inhabitants. Thereafter, it was in no mood to be absorbed by post-war Italy. Italy acquiesced, if grudgingly, in the face of a stalemate that could have been broken only by force of arms. Aosta was granted full autonomy within the framework of the Italian state.

"We do not mind if Italy plays the world diplomatic or political game in our name," explained François. "Who cares what diplomats or politicians do as long as they know enough to leave us be."

Being left to their own devices was still what most of the hundred thousand inhabitants of the Valle wanted. Most were content to go about their age-old businesses: growing mountain grapes, mining marble, raising stock, and — not least — mountaineering. Some of the world's greatest mountain guides come from the Valle, especially from Courmayeur, under the shadows of Mont Blanc.

However, not all Aostans were content with their lot. A coterie of "forward-looking businessmen" saw the future differently. One of the local parties in the election was their creation. It called for closer ties with the outside world and an end to Valle chauvinism.

"They will probably have their way," said François sadly. "Our people resisted invasions by soldiers, but who can resist the invasion of money? The Italians and French have bribed our leaders to let them start building tunnels under Mont Blanc and *le Grand-Saint-Bernard*. Soon a river of trucks and automobiles will come pouring through the Valle. Already land speculation has begun along the route a four-lane *auto-strada* will take. They tell us we will all get rich with all that traffic. Some will undoubtedly get rich. Some will get poor. But the independence of Valle d'Aosta will surely end. *Eh bien*, what can one do?"

———————————————

That night the weather broke and in the morning we heard that ploughs had reached the col of the Great St. Bernard.

It was time for us to go. The brothers gathered in the courtyard to wave us off and to give us a farewell present. It was a short-handled shovel.

"Leave it at the hospice," Domenico told us. "You may not need it but then again you may."

They gave us another parting gift as well. When we stopped that night we found six straw-wrapped bottles of their finest wines in Liz's trunk.

Within ten minutes of leaving Aosta, we were climbing into heavy clouds that dimmed the car lights to a pallid glimmer.

The scenery we *should* have seen must have been spectacular. To the right the Matterhorn, and to the left Mont Blanc. We saw nothing. In second gear, sometimes in first, we groped through an impenetrable murk. So it went for an hour, by which time we had climbed six thousand feet.

Then we emerged between two layers of cloud and could see a little way about us. Behind was the inclined trough of the valley, clogged with roiling clouds. Around us was arctic tundra, barren and rocky, leading the eye to the snowy peaks of mountains on a level with us. Ahead was a wall of rock rising, so it seemed, perpendicular to our path and scarred by a road climbing its face in tortuous switchbacks.

We drove on and the road deteriorated into a track so steep in places that our wheels spun. Watered gasoline reached the carburetor and the consequent lurchings did nothing to ease the strain of manoeuvring along the ledge. Snowbanks appeared and grew deeper until they hemmed us in, sometimes ten feet high. Masses of wet snow slid into the ruts and several times we had to halt and dig our way clear. The murk closed in again and brought with it a driving wind laden with sleet that clogged the windshield wipers.

The desolation seemed absolute until we swung around the last hairpin bend of hundreds and there before us was the striped barrier of the customs post. Seldom have I seen a sweeter sight.

Only one man was on duty, a half-frozen youngster who gaped at us from a face blue with chill then quickly raised the barrier to let us by. He was a realist who understood that passports and papers were meaningless up here.

"Go with God!" he cried, and fled to the shelter of his hut.

We were now on the col at more than eight thousand feet. A gale from Switzerland drove over the pass into our faces. Liz crawled on until the huge grey bulk of the hospice loomed ahead. An unadorned, massive, oblong stone structure five storeys high, it looked more like an enormous barracks than a hospice. It appeared to be abandoned. Nobody answered the heavy door when I pounded on the panels, but it was not locked so we pulled it ajar and went inside. We wandered up and down damp, stone-slabbed corridors, finding no human beings. Finally I summoned the courage to hammer on a heavy bronze bell. The echoes died into silence and we were about to leave that dark and frigid place when a lay brother appeared. He was dwarfed in stature, hard of hearing, and not pleased to see us.

By this time I desired only to be safely down from the pass into springtime again, but Fran was adamant about the dogs. They had brought us this far and we were going to see them. Where were they? The lay brother gestured towards the door but declined to guide us. So we went out into the storm, wondering if we stood a chance of being rescued ourselves if we went over some unseen cliff.

A path marked by a red rope strung on long poles wandered off over the drifts. We followed the markers, sinking knee-deep in wet snow, until we came to a low stone building. The door swung open at my touch but again no human being was there to receive us. The dogs' guardian must have been holed up in the monastery with the rest of his tribe.

Several St. Bernards were curled up in small pens, noses under tails. With some trepidation we walked down the corridor between the cages to the pen of a gigantic beast whose name, according to a tag on his cage, was Barry. Barry woke slowly, peered at us from bloodshot eyes, and laboured to his feet. I reached through the bars and scratched his ears. When I desisted he raised an enormous paw, intimating that I had better scratch some more. I did as he wished, while suggesting that he was a shirker who ought to have been out doing his duty in the storm. He yawned hugely. I was being naïve. His grandfather might perhaps have gone out in weather like this, but those were other days.

We left the icy kennel feeling dispirited, for it was clear that the magnificent dogs of the St. Bernard were anachronisms in this new age, merely objects for tourists to gape at. Even Barry, lineal descendant of the first great Barry, seemed to know this.

We returned to the hospice and, after a great deal of difficulty, managed to find a monk. I explained that I was interested in the story of the place. He was not. He led us into a chill vault that served as a museum and left us there.

The museum offered faded collections of plants, badly stuffed birds, stone implements jumbled in confusion, and a moth-eaten stuffed St. Bernard dog. In addition there were a few faded pictures. One was of the original Barry who, during the first decade of the nineteenth century, was credited with having saved the lives of twenty-two men and women caught by blizzards on the pass. For the rest, only empty collars, cracked with age and green with mildew, hung on a sweating stone wall.

The hospice seems to have been founded around 1050 by a nobleman's son named Bernard who had taken holy orders. In those times the Mons Jovis pass, as the Romans had called it, was the main gateway between western Italy and the lands to the north. Each spring hundreds of Italian farm workers would trek northward over the pass looking for work. When they returned in September storms sometimes caught them en route.

Father Bernard refurbished a refuge hut that had probably stood on the col even before Roman times and, with two or three lay brothers, did what he could to help the migrants.

As the centuries passed, the order took on a life of its own, grew powerful and wealthy, and acquired extensive lands in Switzerland and in the Valle. The priors began to see themselves as temporal lords, and the hospice as a monument to their glory. They raised a mighty building containing more than a hundred sleeping chambers capable of sheltering five hundred people. There were dining halls, kitchens, storage chambers, monks' quarters, a church, and a mortuary in which a hundred frozen corpses could be stored if need be.

There were no rescue dogs until the middle of the seventeenth century when a monk discovered that the local mountain dogs had good noses and could sniff out people buried under many feet of snow. Some were taken to the hospice for rescue work. Not many. Never more than six or seven lived at the hospice at any one time. They saved a good many people, though only a fraction of the numbers claimed for them. Still, the tales told about them became legend, and the hospice became famous for the dogs, and richer for that fame.

It is now many years since they have rescued anyone, but the monks continue to breed them, to kennel club standards, and sell them to dog fanciers abroad.

The gale was growing stronger and the driving snow turning to sleet again. We climbed into the car, turned the heater up full, and tackled the descent.

No road was to be seen, only twin tracks in slippery slush, with high snowbanks caving in on one side and a sheer abyss falling into the clouds on the other. We inched downward. At a sharp turn where I was using the hand brake as well as the foot brake, a monster suddenly appeared before us.

Unable to stop, we slithered slowly forward to come to rest nudging bumpers with a Swiss bus. There was no possibility of Liz backing up to let it by. After a few hopeless attempts at reversing up the slimy track, I gave up.

The bus driver, a wild-eyed man with a wild moustache, thrust his head out the window. His mouth worked but the wind blew the words away. He gestured violently with one hand while, with the other, he threw *his* vehicle into reverse and went careening off down the mountain.

I hoped he had no passengers aboard. I inched forward, expecting to find a hole in the slender guard-rails through which bus and driver had plummeted into eternity, but the bus had halted with its rear end jammed into the snowbank, and the driver, waving his arms like a madman, was motioning me to pass — on the outside.

It was a challenge I could hardly refuse. I passed him with my outside wheels a foot or so from the lip of the abyss. Fran claimed she heard wild laughter, then the bus was gone, and we were alone again.

The rest of the descent was comparatively uneventful. After a time the wind dropped, the cloud thinned, the grade eased, and we found ourselves on a recognizable road. A picture-book alpine valley opened below us and the sun shone. Green meadows spread beside us and pipits flew gaily in their mating dances. The air grew warm and we passed through spring into early summer. Chalets appeared and herds of cows stared with incurious eyes.

Five hours after we had begun the climb we emerged into the broad valley of the Rhône. We stopped the car, got out, and walked up and down on level ground until the feel of it seemed normal. Then we drank some brandy and felt very brave.

Roman Remains

WE had arranged to rendezvous with the Sherwoods in London on the coming weekend so time was now of the essence.

Our return journey across France had its highlights, chief amongst them being a meeting with a crimson slug measuring three inches from nose to tail that attempted to hitch a ride on Liz's bumper. But for the most part we drove either through rain or heavy mist that so obscured the countryside we could have seen little of it, even if high-speed driving had not discouraged sightseeing.

When we reached Boulogne, it was to discover we were a day early for our ferry reservation. The Automobile Association agent at the docks laughed at my confusion. "Ne'er you mind, chum," he said as he shepherded us into line for the next

boat. "You'll be a day older when you die." This gave us something to consider during a very rough crossing.

We lay abed that night at Abbots Barton. Next morning
brought some watery sunlight so we toured Canterbury. A red-
painted steam engine on a plinth caught my eye. Although
the Invictus, built in 1824, was one of the first locomotives to
run in England it looked so similar to present-day English locomotives that, had I been able to make the whistle work, I'm
sure it would have produced the same penetrating and petulant
weeep, weeeeeep.

Debris from the Coronation abounded. A gargantuan
wood-and-paper crown, suffering much from the foul weather, leaned precariously atop a prehistoric mound covering the
bones of neolithic men who had lived and died here four or
five thousand years before England knew itself a nation.

Next day we drove on to London and were welcomed to
George and Shirley's rambling flat. They were expecting anoth-
er visitor — Shirley's uncle Lesley, a sixty-five-year-old ex-
Royal Navy officer, who, having been blinded in the First
World War, became an Anglican clergyman. He was arriving
at Waterloo Station and I volunteered to go and fetch him.

Lesley was not what I expected. I had been thinking in
terms of Goodness and Light in the Face of Terrible Adversity,
but he seemed blissfully unaware that he was an Example. Taking my arm in the crowded station, he observed that the sun
was well past the yard-arm and what did I propose to do about

it? He couldn't see the sun but he had intuition. Over drinks in the nearest pub he told me about his nymphomaniac house-keeper.

"You see, old boy, she has this rather odd idea that love-making can restore one's sight ... stimulates the glands, so she claims. Can't be so, of course, otherwise I'd have more eyes in me head than a fly. Care for another?"

That evening we all attended a party atop a London hos-pital in the living quarters of a woman doctor. Our hostess was a wispy, grandmotherly-looking lady, a gynaecologist by trade, with a passionate interest in exploring a theory that the ancient lineage of every human being can be determined by micro-scopic analysis of body hair. She was soliciting samples from her guests.

"To the loo with you!" she ordered firmly. "I must have samples of your head hair, your moustache, your armpit hair, your chest hair, and your pubic hair."

I met Lesley coming out of the bathroom. He was clutch-ing some folded wisps of toilet paper in one hand and feeling for the corridor wall with the other. I identified myself.

"I say, old chap, do you believe she can actually tell the diff?" he asked.

I was noncommittal.

"Well, we shall see. I found a pinch of Benjamin's hair — he's my old setter, don't you know — in my trouser cuff."

I thought that, if the Anglicans had more clergymen of

Lesley's calibre, they could really give the Romans a run for their money.

Lesley had to catch the 2:00 A.M. train home so we undertook to drive him to the station. Easier said than done. When I tried to manoeuvre Liz out of the hospital car park, it was to find the street jammed solid with unmoving vehicles.

"What the hell!" exclaimed George, and then: "Great God . . . the decoration trippers!"

While we had been partying, London had been invaded by people from all over the British Isles intent on getting a last look at the illuminated Coronation decorations. They had been converging since dusk on motorcycles, in private cars, chartered buses, and vans until, by 10:00 P.M. they had succeeded in paralysing London.

Nothing on wheels could move. Buses packed with tired travellers from Wales, Scotland, and every corner of England stood in the streets like islands in a frozen cataract of lesser vehicles. Abandoning Liz, we walked the few blocks to Edgware Road, the main thoroughfare into the city from the north. Nothing moved there either.

It was an awesome spectacle. Although the English are famed for their patience and good humour, I was nevertheless astonished by their amiability under these singularly trying circumstances. I heard not one impatient car horn. Although passengers in buses and vans looked dreadfully weary, they were "carrying on" without complaint.

Inherent British kindliness was very evident. People walked from immobilized automobiles to the nearest pubs and brought back trays of beer that they distributed to those imprisoned in the buses. I saw a young policeman, exhausted by the hopeless attempt to get the traffic moving, presented with a tot of whisky by the driver of a bus. When the traffic on Edgware Road eventually began to inch forward, and a recalcitrant Morris Minor stalled the whole shebang, a posse of bus and lorry drivers hopped from their vehicles with tool kits in hand and fixed the trouble. They could as easily have pushed the little car onto the sidewalk and left it there. I asked one of them why they didn't do just that, and he replied succinctly, "Cor, laddie, that bloke wants to get home as bad as me."

On Monday our host and hostess were due to fly away — George bound for Calcutta at the controls of a newfangled Comet jet, and Shirley in a Constellation bound for New York. They wanted to know what *our* plans were. When we said we had nothing particular in view, but had had our fill of flux and flow, George suggested we might like to spend a quiet week or two in the west country.

"Take yourselves off to the Cotswolds. It's our favourite part of the world and, Lord knows, we've seen the lot! Make for a little place in Gloucestershire called Wotton-under-Edge and when you get there put up at the Swan. I'll call ahead and let them know you're coming. From Wotton you can hare around in any direction and see Old England *au naturel*, not all tarted up for trippers. A hop back into early days might be just what the doctor ordered."

This sounded like good advice. Farewells between us and the Sherwoods having been said, we set out for the west.

We stopped that night at the Compleat Angler near Marlow on the Thames. Our room looked out over a great weir where I had had an argument with a swan on a misty night in 1942 while navigating a Canadian birch-bark canoe liberated from Lady Astor's boat-house. The swan won, and I had to swim ashore leaving the canoe to go over the weir. This was the same weir that once caused so much distress to the travellers in *Three Men in a Boat* — not to mention the dog.

In the morning we continued westward along the Bath Road before turning north to Bourton-on-the-Water. We stayed that night in a mediocre inn where we were given an attic room from which we could watch busloads of tourists visiting this "typical" Cotswold town.

To keep them happy, the management had built a miniature version of the village. It was extremely realistic, even to a reproduction of the inn with a model of the miniature in its proper place. Wondering how far verisimilitude could be maintained, I got down on my knees and, sure enough, there was a copy of the copy of the copy of the copy.... At this point

Fran took me by the arm and led me away, babbling.

A well-preserved row of three-hundred-year-old stone houses curved by a stream nearby. Each was a masterpiece of intelligent living space, entirely constructed from local materials. The effect was of rural England at its postcard best. It evidently seemed so to a wealthy American who, just after the war, decided to buy the entire row, move it to Massachusetts, and rebuild it there. This bold project came to nothing when the residents refused to sell at any price. According to a portly farmer I met in the Barley Sheaf that evening: "They was of the opinion the Yank was wanting to purchase them as well, and carry them across the water to live among the Red Indians."

Frances had suffered a recurrence of her Parisian ailment this day so after dinner I tucked her into bed and went off to explore the countryside. When I found the Barley Sheaf at an otherwise lonely crossroads high up in the Cotswold hills, I went in for a nightcap.

The saloon bar was empty save for a bibulous gentleman who might have been either a lord of the realm or an undertaker. He took no notice of my arrival so I went through to the public bar. It was a long, stone-walled space with a low ceiling and flagged floors. A fireplace smouldered fitfully in one wall.

The room was full of round-faced, red-complexioned, Gloucestershire countrymen: small holders, tenant farmers, and farm labourers. A battered piano stood at one end of the room and seven or eight young men were grouped around it, forming a wonderful and improbable orchestra. Their chief instruments were a drum made from an old zinc boiler, a corrugated washboard, a bass viol constructed from a tea chest and a broomstick strung with copper wires, three battered hunters' horns, and two sets of bones.

A score of farmers with mugs in hand surrounded the musicians, and while the orchestra worked itself into a perfect frenzy, the onlookers bellowed out both traditional and modern songs.

At the other end of the room, oblivious to the rattle, bang, and blast of the music, dedicated players flung their darts at shredded targets while a half-dozen leathery ancients on a high bench in the gaffers' corner rhythmically tapped their mugs on the tabletop.

No one questioned my alien presence. Someone thrust a pint into my hand and cried in my ear, "Have a go, chum! Come on, have a go!" I was reluctant at first but, after three or four more pints of dark and bitter local ale, found myself on the bass viol.

I let myself go with an abandon I had not felt since the "live, laugh, and be merry" mood of the early war years.

The stentorian voice of the proprietor called the closing mantra, "Time, gentlemen, please," and as he dimmed the lights, I felt something I can describe only as a flicker of heart's ease. Driving back to the hotel I silently blessed George Sherwood.

Wandering on next day we came to an old cemetery of the kind that seems to demand exploration. In it we found the grave of a man named Pearce who had been laid to rest in 1728 at the age of sixty-three. His imposing tomb carried this inscription:

Here lies the Earl of Suffolk's Fool.
    Men called him Dicky Pearce.
His folly serv'd to make folks laugh,
    When wit and mirth were scarce.
Poor Dick, alas! is dead and gone.
    What signifies to cry?
Dickys enough are still behind,
    To laugh at by and by.

Passing through the twin villages of Upper and Lower Slaughter we turned south again. It rained, not heavily, but as though it would never cease.

We were following a remote byway when we came to a little sign pointing up a narrow track towards a dark wall of forest. It was such a modest little sign that I had to pull over and stop in order to read it. All it said was: Roman Villa. Unable to resist such a diffident invitation, we turned up the track into a hidden fold in the hills.

An uneasy mist drifting down from the surrounding ridges obscured a small clearing in the forest where the track ended.

Here, in 1864, two hunters, having lost their ferret down a rabbit hole, were trying to dig him out when they uncovered pieces of Roman paving. This discovery so excited the interest of the landowner, the Earl of Eldon, that he spent the next two decades and a small fortune excavating what proved to be an elaborate complex of ruins.

Some time in the latter part of the second century A.D. an adventurous Roman, perhaps a disbanded legionnaire, had come into this out-of-the-way corner of the Cotswolds seeking a place to settle. In the heavily wooded valley of the Coln he came across a bank of a finely divided clay called fuller's earth, plenty of game, and land that could be easily tilled once the trees had been cut down.

The place suited him and he made a beginning with labour supplied by Celts of the subjugated Dobruni tribe. Land was cleared and rough sheds erected to house a cloth-making works. Fuller's earth from the nearby bank was used to absorb grease and oil in raw wool obtained from Dobruni shepherds on the downs above.

Decades passed and the works flourished, making and dying fine woollen cloth for export to Mediterranean markets. New buildings of carefully cut and mortared stone were added. As the generations passed, the estate became ever more prosperous until, by the middle of the fourth century, it housed and employed as many as a hundred people who laboured in fields and factory for the family of a Romano-British "laird."

Only a few decades later, Rome pulled its garrisons and administrators out of the Province of Britain, leaving the great island to its own devices, which soon amounted to anarchy induced by tribal wars and invading barbarians.

The estate was abandoned. Native Britons used its disintegrating buildings as shelter from winter storms until the roofs and walls collapsed. Then the forests grew back and buried it for more than sixteen hundred years.

What the earl's diggers found was not much more than the floors, with here and there a low section of masonry. Not much . . . yet enough to enable the imagination to envisage what had once been.

Wood pigeons and rooks swept over the clearing and rabbits bounced about on the greensward. Apart from them, Fran and I had the place to ourselves. As we walked slowly through sodden, knee-deep grass and thigh-high brambles, we saw the villa rise again. White-plastered stone buildings with red-tiled roofs surrounded a spacious rectangular courtyard paved with flagstones. The buildings were fronted by pillared colonnades running right around the square.

The master and his family lived in the west wing — a string of a dozen rooms, including a spacious dining and living hall, several bedrooms, lavatories, and, by no means least, the baths.

The baths were the social centre if not the heart of the villa. They included dressing rooms, two hot rooms (one of which served the same purpose as a modern sauna), and a chamber containing a sunken tub large enough to hold several people — a "hot tub" of antiquity.

Furnaces fuelled with charcoal under the masonry floors supplied hot water through an intricate system of lead and clay pipes. The same furnaces heated the living quarters through hot-air ducts built into the walls, a sophisticated and effective central heating system still unmatched in most English homes even in the twentieth century.

The north wing, which extended eastward beyond the square, housed the factory. Here fullers, spinners, weavers, and dyers worked. Those in charge may have been freemen but most of the labourers would have been slaves living in wooden barracks of which no trace now remains. Nonetheless, their ghosts were here. As I looked at elaborate frescoes and mosaics portraying the amusements and entertainments of the élite who had once luxuriated in these baths, my thoughts strayed to the men who had stoked the subterranean furnaces. Who were they? Descendants of the conquered Celts reduced to serfdom? Slaves bought at the nearby market town of Cirencester? Prisoners taken from the rebellious tribes of the northern border country?

The prize relic in the villa's little museum was an intricately carved and curved silver spoon from the cosmetic kit of a Romano-British lady. Pewter replicas of it were for sale. Not for me. I carried away a shard of crude domestic pottery, perhaps part of a labourer's soup bowl, discarded on a spoil heap by the archaeological investigators as being of no consequence.

Under-Edge

WE dropped down into the broad valley surrounding Cirencester, bound for Wotton-under-Edge.

We found Wotton (pronounced Wooton) to be a town of four thousand souls huddled under the edge of the Cotswold escarpment, which here faced westward to the estuary of the Severn River. Although limestone-built and slate-roofed, it did not have the sombre air of most English towns of similar construction. Every house sported a yard full of flowers. The streets were busy and vibrant and the people open and friendly. When I stopped to ask a policeman the way to the Swan, he hopped into the back seat and guided us to it.

The Swan turned out to be a sprawling, pleasantly unkempt hostel dating to the fifteenth century, or earlier. Its proprietor,

Stanley Cooper, was a sleek-haired little fellow with a publican's florid colouring. He and his wife had held the leasehold on the Swan since 1927 and it was, as Stan took pains to impress upon us, "a free public house, and the only one of fourteen pubs in Wotton what is! Free as a bird, me cocky lad!" By which he meant that the Swan was not owned by one of the giant breweries and "let" out to a publican on the infamous tight-hold system.

The Coopers had been expecting us. While a young lad took our luggage up to a lopsided room with a sloping floor overlooking the narrow street, Stan herded us into the bar for an introductory drink. The Swan had only one bar room. "Can't stomach them private bars and lounge bars for the nobs. This is a *public* house with a *public* bar and them as don't like it can go elsewhere."

Leaving his wife, Sar (for Sarah), to take care of business, Stan took us on a tour of the premises. The ancient structure was a warren of dark halls and alleys, permeated with the smell of beer from the cellars and of horses from long empty stables. "Nary hide nor hair of a horse been in the courtyard since before the Queen Mother — God bless 'er — were born. But, as you Yanks like to say, the melody lingers on."

Having observed with delight my reaction to being called a Yank, Stan made a point of continuing to do so. "He'd stir the devil with his own pitchfork just for a lark, would Stan," was Sar's comment.

Stan led us into the garden behind the inn where we were confronted by an enormous tiger upon whose back sat a mangy, chattering monkey. The tiger was stuffed. It was also moth-eaten and rain-soaked, as were the other members (except the monkey) of a menagerie that included a Himalayan bear ("Got 'im from a circus wot was on a train as was into a argyment with another train outside o' Gloucester") and an emu or maybe an ostrich. This was Stan's zoo. "Easier to keep when they're stuffed," he explained. I could not fault his logic.

However, it was not the bedraggled denizens of his zoo he had brought us out to see. It was his tomatoes. Staked against a ten-foot limestone wall that they were overtopping, they sported fruits as big as musk melons.

"Wotcher think?" he asked, his round face beaming with pride.

I said I didn't believe they were tomatoes at all; some exotic tropical fruit, perhaps?

Fran was awestruck. "However did you make them grow like that, Mr. Cooper?"

Stan fairly squirmed with delight. "'Tis *beer*, lass. Worthington's! *And* Bass! *And* Guinness! I saves the slops and regular every day gives me tomatoes a good long drink, which they soaks up like dew!"

Although food rationing was still in effect in England, Sar seemed to know nothing of it. For supper that night she served us vast quantities of roast pork, boiled beef, soggy Yorkshire pudding, boiled potatoes, turnips, cabbage and, for dessert, strawberry tart, and bread pudding soaked in treacle. It sank Fran, who toddled off to bed. It brought me down to my load marks but I remained sufficiently afloat to join Stanley in the bar for a nightcap.

The regulars had gathered. Darts thudded against oaken walls. Reeking pipes made the air dense with swirling fumes. Everyone Stanley introduced me to insisted on buying me a drink, especially Harold Shortt, who was tweedy, amiable, and a connoisseur of esoteric drinks. Maureen, his wife, was willowy and, like her husband, well-informed about Gloucestershire. Over the course of the next two weeks, Harold would introduce Fran and me to such local nectars as mulled cider, barley wine, Welsh mead, and quince brandy. And together, Maureen and Harold would conduct us on a passionate tour through five thousand years of Cotswold history.

Fran and I spent most of the next day on our own, moseying around in the vicinity of Wotton trying to get a feel for the place. From the edge of the escarpment behind the town, we looked westward over a domesticated coastal plain of little villages, squiggly roads, woods, and oddly shaped fields, and beyond them to a vast stretch of salt flats bordering the Severn estuary. The Welsh mountains loomed in the distant north.

At our feet deep valleys, rank with wet woods, sliced into the escarpment. The high plateau rolling eastward behind us was verdant with new wheat and pastures speckled with sheep, and everywhere embossed with beautifully built stone fences. Here and there these ancient walls were crumbling. The art of the dry-stone mason, which had flourished since neolithic times, was dying here in the Cotswolds, as almost everywhere in England.

Turning back, we followed the twisted strand of a one-lane track down a dark valley to the lowlands, then drove eastward past Wotton into a great unkempt tract of land eerily at odds with the generally tailored neatness of the countryside.

This was Tortworth, a six-thousand-acre estate, which, along with the title Earl of Ducie, had fallen only a year earlier to the inheritance of a very surprised young Australian sheep farmer.

George Sherwood had piloted the BOAC flight that brought the new earl to England. Somewhat lost and lonely in "Pommyland," the young man turned to George and Shirley for guidance. George took a week off work to bring the earl "home." The visit began at the Swan and for Stanley Cooper it was memorable.

"When Jarge told me this young fellah he had in tow was the Earl of Ducie come home to his own I thought to meself: Jarge, what kind of a idjit d'you take me for? But I played along. 'Oh, yiss, your Grace,' I says, bowing down nigh to the floor. 'What'll be your Grace's desire? Champagne from Molly's silver slipper?' Molly was our barmaid then. Aye, and it went on from there. It was your Grace this, and your Grace that, and your Grace tiddledy-dee, until I had the whole place roarin'. And that damned Jarge, he never called me off.

"Fortnight later I gets a letter addressed to Mr. Cooper, Publican, and Fool by Appointment. It has the Ducie coat of arms on it and inside an engraved invitation to come and entertain the company when the new earl met his tenantry at Tortworth.

"Did I go? Not bloody likely! It were bad enough being laughed at all over Wotton without half the shire joining in."

The Tortworth estate was slowly but surely returning to wilderness. The doorless parish church had long been given over to the rooks. The once-manicured lawns of the sadly neglected great house had been tunnelled and burrowed into lumpy chaos by legions of rabbits. An air of abandonment overlay the whole of man's works. Beech and oak saplings were sprouting from fields that had not been worked for many years. Farm buildings stood untenanted and often unroofed. We drove through the almost empty "hambletts" of Upper Wick and Nibley Green, where the last private war in England was fought. Maureen Shortt told us that story.

For two hundred years the earls of Warwick and Berkeley had been feuding over the ownership of lands in southern Gloucestershire. Matters came to a head in 1471 when Lord Lisle, an impetuous twenty-year-old of the Warwick line whose seat was Lisle Court in Wotton-under-Edge, challenged William

Berkeley to settle the dispute by force of arms.

William accepted the challenge and rallied five hundred men. On the night of March 19 this private army, equipped with pikes, halberds, swords, and even pitchforks, camped in the Michelwood surrounding Nibley Green, which was to be the field of combat.

Early next morning the impatient Lisle marched *his* force, which also numbered about five hundred, down the hill from Nibley Village. His men were greeted by fierce flights of arrows from the edges of the wood and the battle was on.

News of the challenge had spread throughout the county and beyond, drawing hundreds of onlookers. Some, including children, climbed trees to get a better view of what became a wonderfully bloody show. More than a hundred men fell before James Hiatte, a Forest of Dean archer serving with William, shot an arrow through Lord Lisle's right eye.

With Lisle dead his men lost heart and fled, hoping to take refuge in Lisle Court. Berkeley's men killed many of them during the rout, then sacked and razed the Court. No doubt the audience went home well satisfied with the performance.

It seemed incomprehensible to me that, in this crowded island, such a broad sweep of good, flat land as Tortworth should be effectively abandoned. Yet it was so; though neither then nor later could I obtain a convincing explanation. The best anybody could offer was something to do with legal entanglements.

Whatever hung over Tortworth was too much for the new earl. After spending less than a month with his inheritance, he flew back to Australia and had not been seen since, although George did get a postcard from him. "Picture of a cracking great kangaroo on the front. On the back, fellah had written: 'When Big Reds show up in Tortworth I'll be back. 'Til then good on ye!'"

————————————

The Shortts were waiting in the Swan's bar when we returned to Wotton. "Meaning no disrespect to Sar," Harold murmured over a pint of bitters, "but we thought we'd give your tummies a rest and take you to Hunter's Hall for a bite."

Hunter's Hall was a lonely little inn huddled at a minor crossroad a few miles north of Wotton. It was owned by a London actress and her ex-stockbroker husband who were living the much-cherished English dream of running a country pub.

"It's costing them their shirts," Maureen told us, "but little they care. The locals are on to a good thing. They call Peter 'gaffer' and laugh at all his silly jokes and drink his beer, and forget to pay for it. What odds? He's happy. Pat's happy too. She loves to cook and does a smashing job of it."

Indeed she did. While we ate poached salmon, grouse baked with mushrooms, and chocolate mousse, Maureen and Harold talked about Wotton-under-Edge.

"A thousand years ago Wotton was a thriving little place, making its living out of the wool trade. Fairs for cloth-makers, buyers, and wool merchants were held every summer. They were lively events. Around 1200 one got out of hand and the whole village went up in smoke. Wooton was rebuilt closer to the escarpment and in consequence added 'under Edge' to its name.

"Gloucestershire was getting to be a regular holiday camp for the high and mighty by then. Henry II came here looking for a bit of fluff and found Fair Rosamond, as he called her. Jane Clifford was her proper name. Henry built a love nest for the two of them, 'a house of such wonderful workings that no man or woman might get in to her.' Not content with that, the suspicious old blighter had a high-walled maze built around the place. The story is that when he'd taken a drop or two, even he couldn't find his own way in or out. But his wife, Queen Eleanor, knew a trick of her own. She bribed a servant to show *her* the way in, then she did for poor Rosamond. Made her drink poison.

"Her epitaph tells the sad tale: 'Here Rose the Fair, not Rose the Chaste, reposes. The smell that rises is not the smell of roses.'

"If Henry II lost his light-of-love here, Edward II lost the lot. In 1326 Edward's French wife, Isabella, turned on him. With help from home she unseated the poor old chap. He was hustled to Bradley Court, here in Wotton, then to Berkeley Castle dungeons. Being a weakly chap, it was thought rough treatment would do him in. But he was made of better stuff than his captors counted on. Lack of food; only stone floors to lie upon; a spot of torture now and again (nothing that would leave a mark, mind); and still he kept his pecker up. His jailers lost patience. One September night they tied him face down to a rack and poured molten lead into him through his bottom.

"Lord Berkeley was conveniently out of town at the time — holed up in his manor here at Wotton. When he got the news he hurried home — terribly shocked, of course — to find Edward gone to meet his Maker.

"The bod was examined by a bevy of Berkeley's tame priests who could find not a mark on him. Died of natural causes, they said. Isabella lived happily ever after. So did the Berkeleys, for whom she couldn't do enough."

As we drove back to Wotton, Harold added a snippet to the story. Pointing to a little copse, he said, "The last wolf in Gloucestershire was killed just over there in 1281. Ah, the last *natural* wolf, you might say. There've been packs of the two-legged kind denning in the manors and castles around here ever since. And there're those who'd be happy to trade the lot for the four-legged kind. Perhaps you could send us some from Canada?"

I went to bed that night musing on a Wotton advertisement Fran had seen and noted down for me.

A. Keynton & Son. Builders — Contractors — Decorators

and Complete Undertakers.

The businessmen of Wotton did not do things by halves.

—————————————————

During the days that followed — for the most part grey days with dirty easterly weather — we spent much of our time exploring the countryside with the Shortts. One morning we drove north to Uley Bury. Steep-sided limestone peninsulas jut from the Cotswold plateau towards the Severn River and Uley spur is one of them. Standing eight hundred feet above the river plain, it thrusts to the west like the prow of a titanic ship. Its "deck" encompasses some fifty level acres, and its exceedingly steep slopes are mossed by what remains of ancient forests. Although it is a natural feature, it bears the appearance of being a human construct. Appearances are not entirely deceptive. Human beings have been modifying the spur through five millennia and have succeeded in re-shaping it into a feature that will testify to human obduracy long after the pyramids of Egypt have crumbled into dust.

The carefully levelled crest was cut off from the parent plateau by several deep ditches dug across the neck of the spur. Banked-up soil and rock from these massive excavations formed ramparts that are still fifteen to twenty feet high. On occasion, ditches and banks had been rendered more formidable by adding log walls and rows of sharpened stakes. A narrow path across them had been defended at its outer end by earthwork forts, now reduced to shapeless mounds.

This was the least of what had been accomplished. The upper slopes of the spur had been re-shaped to form two enormous ditches one above the other, each twenty feet deep, combined with three mighty earthen ramparts as high as the ditches were deep.

The quantities of earth and stone that had to have been dug and moved in order to produce this colossal works boggled my mind. And it had all been done by hand, probably without even the assistance of draft animals.

Harold drove the point home. "Friend of mine, engineer wallah, had a look at the old Bury. 'Harold,' he told me later, 'I've made some jottings and unless those blighters had the angelic hosts *and* the devil's minions to lend a hand, they couldn't have built that place in much under a million man hours.' Of course they had neither the one nor the other. What they did have were deer-horn picks, wooden shovels, and baskets they carried on their heads or backs."

The first people to use the Bury seem to have been neolithic pastoralists. Around 3500 B.C. they found the windswept and forest-free crest of the spur a good place to stockade their livestock, probably by means of wooden fencing, or even piles of brush, strung across the neck to keep the stock in and predators out.

For about a thousand years these Stone Age people camped

on the Bury in spring, summer, and fall, descending into the shelter of the forests during hard winters. Then things changed. Mankind made a "great leap forward" by discovering how to smelt and work blends of tin and copper. So the Bronze Age arrived, bringing better tools — and deadlier weapons.

Trouble inevitably followed and people began making use of the Bury as a place in which they could defend themselves against their own kind. Ditches were dug, and banks raised. Nevertheless, the works remained of modest proportions through another millennium, suggesting that war and the rumours of war were still of relatively rare occurrence.

Around 1000 B.C. mankind made another spectacular technological leap by learning to smelt and work iron. The Iron Age seems to have reached Gloucestershire around 700 B.C. It brought in its wake not only even deadlier weaponry but invaders from Europe who knew how to wield iron axes, swords, and spears and had no compunction about doing so.

In their desperate attempts to stem the invasions, the people of the Bury region, who may never have numbered more than a few hundred individuals, lavished almost unimaginable effort on the Bury fortress. It was at this time that the encircling ditch-and-rampart systems were constructed.

By 300 B.C. the enclosure on the crest had become home to a more-or-less permanently beleaguered people. Then they were assailed by a singularly terrible warrior race from across the Channel: the Celts. True products of the Iron Age, the new invaders were fierce conquistadors before whose iron might no Bronze or Stone Age people could long survive.

The Celts stormed Uley Bury and, if they ran true to form, slaughtered the male defenders, seized the women and cattle, and occupied the lands and habitations.

Although the Celts reaped rich rewards for being at the leading edge of the technology of their times, there was a price to pay. Weapons designed to kill an enemy inevitably turn upon those who wield them. The Celts turned upon each other. They refurbished and enlarged the ancient hill fortresses, converting them into tribal strongholds from which they raided other Celts in neighbouring hill forts. Uley Bury acquired new ditches, ramparts, and walls of stone and timber.

The Celts did not long remain at the forefront of civilization. Shortly after the beginning of the Christian era, the Romans invaded England. The Celts fought furiously but were militarily outclassed. One by one their hill forts were assaulted by Roman legions equipped with giant catapults and other deadly inventions. One by one the forts were taken and the defenders put to the sword.

Thereafter, most of the hill forts, Uley Bury amongst them, were abandoned by all but shepherds and farmers, whose ploughs still turn up artifacts from those earlier times when men sought sanctuary from their fellows here.

We picnicked in the shelter of a gatehouse mound, then Fran and the Shortts catnapped in the pale sunshine while I went wandering. "Mind you keep your eye peeled for adders," Harold warned me. "Little devils'll be out looking for a bit of sun themselves. Harmless, of course, if you don't step or sit on them."

I met no adders, but as I climbed to the highest part of the ramparts I did meet a fox, who gave me a casual wave of his tail.

I looked northwest across the good farmland of the valley, and beyond the muddy-hued Severn estuary to the distant Welsh mountains. Snowdon, the highest peak in Britain, was a vague presence on the farthest horizon. To the south, I could see the grey void of the Bristol Channel and the Exmoor hills of Devon. Southeast lay the chalk cliffs of Wiltshire. Bursts of watery sunshine swept over this magnificent panorama illuminating distant details — a fishing vessel ploughing the estuary; a glitter of wet slate roofs from a village far to the northwest; and that latest manifestation of civilization — fighter jets swarming from an airfield near the smoky sprawl of Bristol.

Close at hand was a tumbledown hut sheathed in galvanized iron. It seemed an atrocity in such a place, and when I rejoined the rest of the party I complained about it.

"An observer corps post during the war," Harold explained. "Fellows used to perch up there night and day listening and looking for Jerry planes. Did it myself after I was mustered out. I was up here one moonlit night when Jerry bombed Bristol. A sight I won't forget. Whole damned place looked to be going up in flames. Searchlight beams thick as hedgehog quills. Ack-ack flying about thick as rain. A stick of bombs fell straight across Wotton; blew up half a dozen houses. Towards the end a Jerry pilot jettisoned a big one and it crashed down right into the Bury. Like a bloody earthquake, it was. Scared the lights out of us though it hurt nobody except rabbits.

"Ah, yes, this old Bury has seen some queer sights in its time. And I don't doubt, given the nature of the beast, it'll see some more."

"The beast?" Fran asked.

"The two-legged one, Frances, me dear. The two-legged one, don't you know?"

_____

The fog closed in as we drove away from the Bury past a massive mound on the lip of the escarpment, surrounded by newly ploughed red earth.

Maureen did not wait for my question. "That's Hetty Pegler's Tump. Hetty was a naughty girl who had intercourse with the devil — a *Protestant* devil — back in Bloody Mary's time and got herself burned at the stake for her trouble. But, of course, it's really a prehistoric long barrow — a tumulus. Very, very old . . . and very, very spooky. We can't visit it today because we'd sink up to our ears in mud. Besides, it's opening time at the pub."

Late on an afternoon two days later Fran and I returned to Hetty's Tump. We drove to it along the edge of the escarpment over a vast, windswept common grazed by stocky Cotswold sheep. As instructed, we stopped at a lonely farmhouse half a mile away. In answer to my knock, a harassed-looking woman produced a great iron key and a saucer holding a stub of candle.

"That'll be tuppence each," she said shortly, "and mind you lock the door behind you!"

The chill wind blew rain into our faces as we trudged across the sodden plough. Cloud scud had descended almost to eye level, veiling an oval-shaped mound about 150 feet long by 100 wide and perhaps 20 high. We passed through a squealing gate in a rusted iron fence to reach a heavy wooden door sunk between two monoliths in the south side of the tumulus.

The key worked stiffly. I swung the door ajar, to be faced by a black aperture two feet square, capped by a massive stone lintel. I lit the candle and we crawled in. The floor was earthen and the air smelled of mould. In the flickering candlelight we could make out irregular limestone slabs roofing the narrow tunnel and brushing against our heads. They rested — none too securely, it seemed to me — on drystone walls or upright slabs.

The corridor narrowed, widened a little, sank, and lifted for fifty or sixty feet before bringing us to a pair of empty chambers about six feet square, each capped by enormous single slabs that must have weighed six or seven tons. There was still no room to stand upright and we were feeling definitely claustrophobic, so we reversed direction. Fran kept crowding from the rear, plaintively urging me to hurry up. We were thankful to emerge into the last of the daylight, duly remembering to close and lock the little door behind us.

We had made a very short journey in space, but had travelled some fifty centuries in the course of fifty feet.

Burial mounds concealing chambered tombs are found all over the British Isles. Most were built during the centuries just before or after 3000 B.C. Early antiquarians assumed they were the tombs of individual kings or mighty chieftains. In fact, they most usually housed the remains of a succession of tribal leaders and elders who had died over a span of many hundreds of years.

The enormous expenditure of time and energy required to construct such tombs bears eloquent testimony to the respect and regard the ancient people had for their ancestors — a respect that still exists amongst the few tribal people surviving into our times. It was and always has been an attitude contributing greatly to the cohesion and endurance of society, not just from generation to generation, but from century to century and beyond.

In 1821, when Hetty's Tump was first excavated, the remains of twenty-six human beings were found in its two intact chambers, together with the bones of wild boars and a scattering of flint tools. At least three other chambers once existed but have long since collapsed.

"We've tried to trace what happened to the bones," Maureen told us. "They seem to have been mostly skulls. Probably ended up in a rubbish tip. At least the rest of the old folks who were buried there are still lying where their people put them. God rest 'em!

"I'll tell you another queer thing about Hetty's Tump. Just before the war some rabbit hunters digging into the top of the mound unearthed a human skeleton — buried standing up. The story goes that in the mid-1800s there was a countryman — a poacher, if you like — living like a badger in the woods below the tump. The local vicar, a do-gooder type, tracked him down one day and tried to persuade him to give up his vagabond ways and move into an almshouse down in Uley where he could be looked after and decently buried when the time came.

"The old chap wasn't having any. He told the vicar he was bound to stay where he belonged — that he *belonged* in Hetty's Tump.

"Eventually he disappeared. Harold and I think he dug his own grave — straight down; carried away and hid the surplus soil; then, when his time came, lowered himself into the hole and pulled a sod over his head. It was just rotten bad luck that he was found, and his poor old bones shovelled out to be dumped into a pauper's grave in Wotton."

Valley of Dead Dreams

ONE evening over hot toddies in the Swan's bar, Harold offered us a choice for the morrow.

"Farleys End . . . or Woodchester. Which'll it be?"

"I don't like the sound of Farleys End," I said. "But tell me more."

"Little crossroad village of thirty or forty souls on the Severn flats east of Gloucester. Don't know how it got the name but Farley's a common enough one in these parts. Actually not much to see. Maureen thought you might like to take a gawk anyway, in case you wanted to reserve a plot in their parish cemetery."

"Thanks," I said. "I'll pass. What about Woodchester?"

"Ah, now, that you will just have to find out for yourself."

It threatened rain next morning as we drove across the plateau to the edge of the escarpment a couple of miles past the Uley spur. Below us lay a broad forest-filled valley hardly marred by signs of human presence. The one notable exception was a scattering of limestone buildings crouched at the line of demarcation between the forest's edge and the foot of the scarp's steep slope.

"That's Nympsfield. And all those woods beyond, two thousand acres of them, belong to Woodchester," Maureen explained. "But do look closely at the village. See anything odd about it?"

It took only a moment to spot the peculiarity. "Almost every house is in the shape of a cross! How come?"

"Because they're all RCs," Harold explained. "Papists — and Elizabethan papists at that. Woodchester's like a little papal duchy buried in the heart of Protestant England, one that's three hundred years out of step. The inmates seldom go outside the gates. Rest of the world seldom goes inside. Too bloody weird in there."

At his direction I turned off the single-lane paved road onto a rutted dirt track.

"Have to use the back way in. Main gates are four miles away but so rusty it takes three men and a dog to open them."

Cautiously I eased Liz over the edge of the scarp and shortly drove into the grounds of a mansion set on a broad ledge part way down the slope. Stone-built in Gothic style, it was wonderfully ornate but in a sad state of decay. Mullioned windows were patched with tape. Roof tiles were loose and many had fallen. On the unkempt lawns lay two rubber assault boats of a kind I had last seen during river-crossing operations in the war. Nearby were piles of nylon rope with grapnels attached, a diver's suit, and cylinders of air.

I glanced at the building and saw three boys staring back through grimy windows. One of them drew his finger across his throat . . . and grinned.

"What *is* this place?" I asked.

Maureen smiled wryly. "It's *called* the Cottage — though it's got thirty-odd bedrooms. It's been a lot of things since old William Leigh — who, you might say, is the grey eminence of Woodchester — built it a century ago. It was to be his temporary residence while he was building a proper home down there in the valley. For a time after the First War it was a refuge for monks from Europe. Then it was an Ursuline convent, though Uley folk, good Church of England all, claim it was *both* at the same time. During the last war it was full of secret-weapons boffins. Now it's a sort of boys' school run by a very odd couple from London. Only about a dozen students, so I'm told. But I'm blessed if I know what that stuff on the lawn is all about."

Harold had scrambled out of the car and gone to rap on an iron-studded door in an arched entrance. It was opened by an emaciated-looking man with a bushy head of white hair. After a few words with him Harold returned to the car.

"Rotten bad luck. One of the students — lad from India — drowned in the lake down there last week. Navy frogmen've been looking ever since but haven't found a trace. Well, down we go; but easy, Farley me lad."

Liz slipped and slithered on down into Nympsfield and we drove through its sombre, single street, seeing few signs of life. A woman in a doorway stared at us blankly. A dog snarled at the car, then fled. The track ended just beyond the village. We left Liz and followed a footpath for half a mile through forest as dense and dripping as a tropical jungle, to emerge at the edge of a long clearing. Harold stopped and with a melo-dramatic gesture pointed down the opening.

"Well, there she be! Woodchester House! You ever see anything like that before?"

What Fran and I saw was a lumpen mass of masonry four and five storeys high that seemed to be part fortress, part palace, part cathedral. A jumble of square, round, and octagonal towers bound together by heavily buttressed walls, it had the intimidating presence, though none of the unity of form, of a truncated Mayan pyramid. Its discoloured limestone walls were randomly pocked by scores of windows, no two of them identical. The stepped, flat roofs were edged by castellated parapets above which towered a forest of chimney pots, some tall enough to be mistaken for factory chimneys.

The answer was no. Fran and I had never seen anything like this before.

We walked towards it knee-deep in wet grass across a meadow where no cattle grazed. Arched windows empty of glass monitored our approach then, as we drew close, vomited black outpourings of rooks. The birds swirled overhead, raucously protesting our arrival.

"My God!" I exclaimed. "What next? A cloud of vampire bats? This is straight out of Dracula!"

Harold shook his head. "It's straight out of William Leigh."

All doors and windows in the first floor had been walled shut, but Harold led us around to the rear where there was a breach. Entering, we found ourselves in a labyrinth of stone-arched cellars.

Although the external and internal walls of the building had mostly been completed, the structure was largely a shell. I could look up through five non-existent floors until my sight wavered amongst the distant beams that took the great weight of the roof. It was like gazing up through a giant elevator shaft for, at each level there were doorways. The effect was made more bizarre by vertical rows of fireplaces built into the thick stone walls and never darkened by so much as a puff of smoke.

I had the uncanny feeling that this place had been built for aerial beings, and the fantasy strengthened as a flock of jackdaws wheeled in through a gaping upper window, swung down into inner space, and dispersed to their nests in fireplace openings and on unfinished cornices.

We climbed a stone ramp designed to carry a staircase and

found ourselves balancing on rough-cut planks between arches intended to support non-existent floors. Bearing stones were traced with chalk marks showing how they had been shaped. Keystones were set into arches so neatly not even dust could filter down between their joints. We came across masons' hammers and chisels where they had been laid down when work had ceased. Vast stocks of cut stone were stacked in the cellar crypts along with templates and patterns for decorations that had never been carved.

We moved cautiously through this skeletal structure. Temporary plank flooring had been laid here and there, along which we made our way by guess and by God. The place was enormous. There could not have been fewer than a hundred rooms planned on the four main levels, not to mention the attics, which would have been filled with servants' quarters.

A circular stone stairway pierced the entire structure. It opened into a tower containing the rusted mechanism of a huge clock, topped by an immense bell. No rope hung from the bell, which appeared fixed on its trunnions, but Harold told us that on days and nights when winter gales roared the bell swung free and its voice boomed out over the valley.

Almost every room had its fireplace, each a beautiful example of the stonemason's art. The maze of flues running through the thick walls must have been of incredible complexity.

We found our way into the chapel, which was as large as many a church. A choir loft hung thirty feet above the nave, opposite a complex of stained-glass windows fifty or sixty feet high by at least thirty broad that would have done credit to any cathedral in Christendom. Most of the windows now hung twisted and broken on their intricate traceries of lead, and the floor below was littered with multi-coloured shards of glass.

Gingerly we made our way along a second-storey hallway whose "floor" was the arched stonework of a hall beneath. Some of the rooms leading off it had been partially floored, and they contained an astonishing miscellany of objects. In one, partly buried under half-a-century's accumulation of bird droppings and old nests, was a beautifully detailed doll's house. Skeletonized rooks crunched underfoot in others. A layer of guano coated a huge dynamo that seemed as out of place in this antique setting as a television set. It may have been brought by American army units who briefly attempted to make use of the place during the war. The military had left signs of their presence. Pornographic couplets were scrawled on the walls of some of the rooms and the ubiquitous "Kilroy was here" had been scratched into the smooth face of a marble pediment.

We met no living soul nor saw any recent signs of life, except for the dog. We were carefully traversing a partly completed corridor when a small, soft-eyed spaniel appeared. It came up to us and passed by without glancing in our direction — treating us as if we did not exist. Later we came across its home in one of the lower rooms, where it had made a bed in a litter of old rooks' nests. Where the creature came from and what its life was in this abandoned ruin we could not guess.

High up under the attic beams was a cavernous chamber of inscrutable design. Great marble hearths reached by stone stairs over arched bridges were set against one wall. The several levels in this great room each had its mysteries. On one stood an oblong stone structure some ten feet long by six broad. It looked like nothing so much as a giant's coffin, except that its top was a one-piece stone tray pierced by drain holes at both ends. Not even Harold could hazard a guess as to its purpose. This room was full of bats, which perturbed the ladies. Maureen led a retreat to the out-of-doors.

The rain had diminished to a wet haze so we elected to walk a little farther up the valley through a lush, untrammelled growth of shrubbery and meadow. Rabbits and birds watched us fearlessly as if man's presence was alien here.

The sound of car engines startled the animals and us. A navy truck carrying several divers ground towards us and passed by. Behind it came an open jeep, in the back seat of which sat a dark-skinned, sad-faced man. He raised his hand almost imperceptibly towards his turban as he passed.

The rain began again. To our left a jungle of entwined trees obscured the black, weed-covered surface of the lake. Ropes had been stretched across it to mark the limit of that day's search.

When we climbed back up to the Cottage, the schoolmaster emerged to tell us that the body had not yet been found and that one of the navy divers had nearly drowned when his oxygen apparatus failed.

We were more than a little subdued as we drove back to the Swan late that afternoon. It was not until we had dined well at Hunter's Hall and were comfortably settled in a fire-lit corner of the saloon bar that the Shortts felt up to telling us about Woodchester.

The Woodchester story is about possession.

There may have been earlier victims of the "Woodchester malady," as Harold phrased it, but the first of whom there is any record was a third-century Roman who must have been a man of great wealth and power. For reasons we will never know, he chose this sequestered, thickly forested valley cleaving into the Cotswold plateau as the place to leave his mark. Here, on the outer edge of Empire, he built a mansion on such a grandiose scale that even the emperor Constantine is said to have been a guest within its walls.

This palace in the wilderness appears to have survived for more than a hundred years, but some time after the collapse of Rome in Britain, it was sacked and levelled to the ground. It did not re-enter human ken until late in the sixteenth century, when the Woodchester parish cemetery was being extended. A gravedigger's spade brought up a scattering of brilliantly coloured tesserae, the tiny, glazed-clay building blocks of Roman mosaics. As new graves were dug over the succeeding years, more tesserae appeared and were given to children to play with. It was not until 1793 that an antiquarian became interested enough to undertake an excavation. His work revealed one of the finest Roman mosaics ever found in Britain. It covered the floor of a splendid dining hall in a palatial courtyard building. What little has since been excavated suggests that this villa was of a size and magnificence unparalleled in Britain, and not overmatched by many elsewhere in the Roman Empire.

"The villa looks to have been the first Great House the valley conjured up," said Harold. "There's no way of telling when the next one came along but Woodchester's name comes straight from the Saxon *udecastre*, which means castle, or mansion, in the woods. One of the Saxon invaders must have built a mansion here after the Romans were gone. And it must have been some place to've kept the name alive a thousand years and more!"

When the Danes arrived, about A.D. 1000, Earl Godwin, the Saxon lord of the region, saw the handwriting on the wall and allied himself with the Danish invaders by marrying Gytha, a Christian woman of Danish royal blood.

Things did not go smoothly for him on the domestic front. A nunnery near what would one day be Berkeley village owned some rich fields that Godwin coveted. Disguising an effeminate nephew as a girl, he sent the lad to the nunnery to plead for sanctuary. The youth was admitted and was sheltered for some months by the unsuspecting women. Meanwhile the earl spread rumours that the nuns were harbouring a man "for their pleasures" and in due course led an angry mob to investigate. The nephew was exposed (and duly rewarded); the nunnery was broken up; and Godwin got the lands.

But he lost his wife's favour. She was so shamed by the insult to the church that thereafter she refused to live on or eat anything grown on soil owned by her husband. To placate her, the earl bought Woodchester in her name and built for her there a mansion that was reputedly the envy of Harthacanute, then the Danish king of England.

A son called Harold was born to Godwin and Gytha in the "great house fit for a king." As a consequence of considerable conniving by his father, Harold grew up to become king of England, only to die in 1066 on the field of Hastings.

To the victors go the spoils. William the Conqueror gave Woodchester to one of his Norman knights, Edward of Salisbury. The gift brought no luck. Edward's line ended with the death of *his* son in another of the interminable wars of the times.

"Woodchester wasn't what you'd call a lucky place," said Harold, taking a thoughtful sip of the whisky I had just bought him. "The great Godwin mansion went the way of the rest. Disappeared. Nobody even knows now where it stood. And, if the Salisburys built one of their own, it too left no trace."

For centuries the Catholic church had been amassing land all over England, and by 1300 was in possession of most of the valley. A small part, however, was held by a family named Maltraver, who were devoted servants of the Church. One of the regicides who helped dispose of Edward II at Berkeley Castle in 1327 in order to seat a Catholic queen on England's throne was Baron John Maltraver of Woodchester.

"The Maltravers got their reward," Harold told us. "Land and money. But they also contracted the Woodchester malady, and went ahead hog-wild and built a mansion that was the envy of lay and spiritual lords alike, which was their bad luck, for they were only small fry amongst the bigwigs of the times. They were accused of heresy, there was a fight, their big house burned to the ground, and their land was seized by the high and mighty Earl of Arundel."

Arundel demolished what remained of the Maltraver manor and erected an even grander one in its stead. His family shared the valley with the Benedictines until Henry VIII repudiated Roman Catholicism and seized Woodchester for the king. Sir Thomas Arundel was burned at the stake along with two other loyal Catholics, leaving this dying protestation:

> Theis iii knyghtes confessyed that they war never gylte
> for sich thynges as was laid unto thier charge, and so dyde
> in that same opinoun.

The Woodchester branch of the Arundel line perished with

Sir Thomas, and shortly thereafter the family seat was fired, whether by accident or malice is not known.

By 1600 the estate, now reunified into one holding of about three thousand acres, was in the hands of the protestant Ducie family, who were at first content to build themselves a rather modest Elizabethan manor.

However, in 1740, Sir William Ducie, who had amassed great wealth from the East India Company, decided to raise a mansion to rival any in the kingdom. He spent the rest of his life at the task and poured all his fortune into it. As he grew old, he became convinced that outsiders were conspiring to prevent him from completing the vast pile. So he built a high stone wall enclosing the entire estate, including the village of Nympsfield. Only one road now entered the valley, and it was guarded by a fortified gatehouse and a forbidding set of iron gates.

When William died he left the task of completing the great house to his son but failed to leave him the wherewithal to do it. Saddled with this incubus, the young man fled, eventually finding his way to Australia. Woodchester then passed to the collateral branch of the Ducie family, which already owned the great Tortworth estate and was wise enough to leave Woodchester to its own devices.

For more than half a century the abandoned mansion stood untenanted while most of the valley reverted to meadow and spreading forest.

Then came William Leigh.

Not even Harold knew much about Leigh's early years except that he was the single-minded son of a mill hand from the industrial north, who was determined "to get ahead."

"As I make him out, he grew up to be the spitting image of the money-grubbing, self-made Bounderby chap old Charlie Dickens flayed in *Hard Times*," Harold told us. "Made pots of money supplying the army and navy with everything from uniforms to cannon turned out in his own sweatshops.

"By the 1840s he'd squeezed as many millions out of north-country labour and out of government contracts as he could, so off he went to Australia to see what he could pick up there.

"Something strange happened in Australia. Might have met a woman he couldn't get round any other way. Anyhow, he converted and became a Roman, built a cathedral in Melbourne that cost half a million, and then got married in it.

"But Down Under didn't suit him. He'd had pots of filthy lucre but, like the nouveau riche from the beginning of time, he wanted to put one in the eye of those he'd left behind, while catching the eye of the nobs.

"What he wanted was a title. He could have bought one — they *are* for sale, you know — only he'd dirtied his copybook. England was Protestant, and not even Croesus could have bought a peerage if he'd been R.C. Leigh tried and got turned down, and that must have been the first time as a

grown man he failed to get something he'd set his heart on.
It changed him.

"He had his agents shop around until they found Woodchester and in 1847 he bought the place.

"What was his intention? Well, if he couldn't become a
lord of the realm, he'd become a lord of the Holy Roman
Church. There's no doubt he believed a return to medieval
Catholicism would produce the kind of world he wanted. It's
my opinion he came to think all England would follow if he
set the right example. What he made of Woodchester was going
to be the example that would start England on the path back
to feudalism and to Rome."

Leigh's first Woodchester project was to build and endow
the Church and Priory of the Enunciation, which is described
as "one of the most beautiful and costly Roman Catholic
churches in Britain, and is associated with one of the most
extensive recent monasteries."

Leigh turned this complex over to the black-robed Domini-
can order, whose first task was to convert to Catholicism the
four hundred inhabitants of the estate.

"The people didn't have the devil of a lot of choice," said
Harold. "Leigh was running the place like one of the old
demesnes. Only he had freehold, so he could chase off any poor
sod who didn't knuckle under. If families refused to convert,
the bailiff sent them packing, leaving homes and fields they'd
lived in and tilled for generations. So most chose to kiss the

crucifix. This was the first step. The next was to rebuild and raise the old stone wall around the estate to isolate the new converts. Then, with a monastery at one end of the valley, Leigh built a nunnery to cork the other end."

Things were beginning to take shape, and it was the shape of the cross. Leigh even had most of the houses in Nympsfield rebuilt in cruciform style. There remained the question of where the Lord of the Demesne would live.

"The half-built Ducie mansion was still there but was a Protestant red rag to Leigh. He had it torn down and the very ground rooted up so as to leave not a trace. Meantime, he'd hired a Parisian architect to design a knock-out of a manor, or castle, or whatever, that would be the most elaborate built in Britain since Buckingham Palace. How big was it going to be? Well, you've seen the part that *did* get built. That's only about half what was in the plans. He'd got the Woodchester malady good and proper!

"He insisted the basic materials had to come off the estate. That meant opening a quarry, building a brickyard and a lime kiln, and setting up a sawmill and an iron smithy. It was all taking the devil of a time, and when the architect estimated it'd take a quarter century to complete, Leigh decided he needed a place to live in for the interim so he built the Cottage, a mansion in its own right perched where he could overlook the rise of Woodchester House down below.

"Monarch of all he surveyed!

"That's surely how he fancied himself. A feudal lord, near as could be. He did his best to keep 'his people' from straying off the estate and getting contaminated. Built them a feed mill. A brewery. A workmen's club. Printed a newspaper — the *Nympsfield Gazette*. Brought in a resident quack for them. Built a cloth mill so's they could make their own clothing. Every Boxing Day he'd sit in front of the pub — the Crown and Rose — and they'd all file by and pull their cowlicks, and pay their tithes, and get a pint of beer for a receipt. And all the while the Black Friars kept the people's souls from straying."

A platoon of stonemasons was brought from Italy to supervise the translation of Leigh's dreams into reality. Woodchester men became, in effect, indentured labour, probably not so very different from those who sweated to raise the pyramids. There were never fewer than fifty employed at any one time and they were paid twelve to fifteen shillings a week — the equivalent of fifteen to eighteen 1953 dollars.

Residents of the neighbouring hamlets of Uley, Stanley, Cam, and Horsley found themselves increasingly estranged from the now-seldom-encountered inhabitants of Woodchester. Leigh's mania was raising a higher wall than his masons could have built.

The years tolled by. Although the vast pile on the valley floor grew slowly, the costs soared swiftly to astronomical levels. The stained-glass windows of the chapel alone cost over sixteen thousand pounds — about a quarter million 1953 dollars.

William Leigh, his wife, three sons, and two daughters, together with their private chaplain and a company of servants, continued to live in the Cottage. As the nineteenth century drew towards its end, William entered his dotage. Nevertheless, he remained as committed to his fantasy as he had ever been. Assisted by his chaplain, he extracted from his three sons (who were by now grown men) the most solemn promises that they would complete what he had begun.

And then he died. He lies in a vault below the south aisle of the cathedral church he built. A larger-than-life, horizontal monument of alabaster, richly carved in antique style, depicts him lying in state, dressed in his robes as a Knight of St. Gregory. On his stone breast sits an intricately carved marble model of Woodchester House.

When his will was read, it was found that most of his once-colossal fortune had been consumed by the monster in the valley. Frank, the eldest son, made a futile attempt to continue his father's work on what had long since become known to the outside world as Leigh's Folly, but he soon fled into the priesthood. He died a few years later in a mental asylum.

The second son, Albert, made his own brief trial but only succeeded in wasting what was left of the family fortune. He fled to the army, was cashiered for drinking, and died in poverty.

Vincent, the youngest son, then inherited the estate and tried to escape by selling it for a mere twenty thousand pounds.

When his sisters frustrated the sale, he killed himself — at the age of thirty-seven.

The sisters, Blanche and Beatrice, spent the remainder of their spinster lives doing good works amongst the Nympsfield villagers, while all about them the colossal delusions of a dead man crumbled into ruin. In 1914 the sisters died and the Leigh line ended.

So also did the dream of Rome reincarnated in Gloucestershire. The Black Friars departed for new homes in Europe and in due course were followed by the Franciscan nuns.

The valley that had absorbed the vitality and wealth of so many for so long was then purchased by a company that operated hospitals for the insane.

The hospital company planned to complete Woodchester House and turn it into the largest and most luxurious private mental hospital in Europe. Had the plans been implemented they would have cost more than one million pounds.

They came to nothing. The company held title for twenty years then went bankrupt. Rooks and bats continued to live undisturbed in the empty rooms of Leigh's Folly and, for all I know, still do.

Harold went to the bar and returned with nightcaps of mulled cider.

I had a question. "You've mentioned the Woodchester malady a good few times, but you've been pretty vague about it. Care to elucidate?"

Harold lowered his mug and grinned.

"Would have thought it was clear enough . . . even to a colonial. It's the disease as makes chaps think they can leave a mark on the world that'll keep their memory alive forever. It's what makes your industrial emperors, business barons, press lords, gold-grubbing bankers, Hitlers, Mussolinis, and the like, swell up like toads with gas on their bellies, growing bigger and bigger until they get too big for their britches. Then, of course, they bust . . . leaving a hell of a mess and a bloody bad smell. Neither of which, thank God, lasts for ever. Nothing does. Which is what the poor sods don't seem to understand.

"Got it now, Farley? If not, perhaps old Percy Shelley can make it clear. You remember the lines?

'My name is Ozymandias, king of kings:

Look on my works, ye Mighty, and despair!'

Well, most people don't recall what follows.

'Nothing beside remains. Round the decay

Of that colossal wreck, boundless and bare . . .'"

The owner of the Hunter interrupted by tapping his little bell.

"Time, gentlemen, please!"

Peter and the Birds

ALTHOUGH our time abroad was drawing to an end, the Shortts weren't yet finished with us.

"You've seen a deal of what went on in these parts in the dim and distant," said Harold one evening at the Swan. "Maureen and I think you ought to see another side before you flit. One that ought to be to your taste. We'd like to take you down to Slimbridge tomorrow to visit Peter Scott."

"Peter Scott? Son of the Antarctic explorer?"

"Aye, that's the lad. Different breed from his old dad, but he does big things too."

We were away at eight, after Sarah Cooper had stuffed Fran and me with porridge and clotted cream, and scrambled eggs accompanied by fried kidneys, sausages, and tomatoes. As we waddled out the door of the Swan, Sar thrust a bulging sack upon us. In response to a questioning glance from me, she smiled and said, "Gie un to Harold. He'll find a use for un."

Harold and Maureen were waiting in their sedate old Ford Pilot. They drove us by way of Dursley, sprawled in the bottom of its own valley a mile from Uley. Although a quiet little village now, Dursley once had a large and lurid reputation. As late as the mid-eighteenth century it boasted two breweries and fourteen pubs for a population of under a thousand and was known throughout the shire as Drunken Dursley.

It did not rank high in the estimation of travellers. John Jackson, a Yorkshireman who had to spend a January day and night in the place in 1756, wrote in his diary:

> In this town I saw two swine killed and burnt as black as a Toad, and one lay on a table, the other ith'i left in its own mucky miry way, ye ugliest object I thought yt ever my eyes beheld; and that more of their cookery is more proper for dogs and swine than men. Their Toad-back bacon and Cabbage-kettle stinking porrage like Traynoil or like the stink of ye Hog Sty.

Maureen explained that Toad-back bacon consisted of slabs of fat sow-belly "cured" in the chimney until it resembled toad skin on the outside. The inside tended to be green and cheesy. The Cabbage-kettle was a pot kept simmering on the open fire and replenished now and again with scraps of vegetables, meal, and meat. Traynoil, or train-oil, was whale, seal, or fish oil, usually rancid. Maureen's description of these viands was so vivid that Fran rolled down the window on her side and thrust her head out into the cool, clean airstream.

Now Harold turned west towards the Severn. Soon we were wobbling along a dirt track across a vast, rain-sodden, estuarine plain on which stood the hamlet of Slimbridge. Its half-dozen grey stone buildings seemed mired in time and far lonelier than any cloud. Beyond it a seemingly endless salt marsh swept to the muddy tidal flats of the Severn. This was Peter Scott's domain.

Born in 1909, Peter had been only four years old when his famous father, Robert Falcon Scott, perished while returning from his epic journey to the South Pole. During his childhood Peter had found himself isolated from his contemporaries by the towering presence of a dead hero. As I myself had done in my time, Peter turned to the world of birds, especially waterfowl, seeking companionship and solace. By the time he was twenty-nine, he had become well known for his haunting paintings of ducks, geese, and swans.

Then the war came. He served through it with the Royal Navy, mostly in the "little ships" — motor torpedo boats, mine sweepers, and the like — where he encountered his fair share of death and destruction.

Although an avid hunter before the war, Peter wanted no more of killing after it. In 1946 he leased twenty acres of prime waterfowling ground from the Berkeley estate, whose lords had used the vast salt marshes called the Dumbles as a private hunting preserve through five centuries. On this little patch of sodden land, Peter set himself to the task of saving what he could of an avian world that had been decimated, not by the guns of war but by the guns of "sportsmen." Here he founded a sanctuary called the Severn Wild Fowl Trust, unique in its time and still an extraordinary venture.

At the time of our visit, Peter was living with his wife and son in a farm worker's cottage crammed with his books and paintings. The family was at breakfast when Harold knocked on their door. The Scotts could hardly have been pleased to see visitors at such an hour, but when Peter heard my name he thought a moment, then shook my hand warmly, and invited us in.

"I've got your book, you know. I was in your part of the Arctic just two years after you. A bit farther north — on the Perry River — looking for Ross's geese. John Ingebritson at Churchill told me about your penchant for running around with wolves. I'm afraid we've no wolves here, but welcome to the Trust."

Peter had a high-domed forehead, receding hairline, and an engaging smile. While his wife poured tea, I told him something about our journey, now almost concluded.

"Jolly good thing you came along here before you went off home. You know about birds, and how badly things are going for a lot of them — especially the waterfowl. So it'll be a delight to show you what we're trying to do about it."

He took us first to the so-called Big Pen, an acre of meadow enclosed by a waist-high wire mesh fence. It was aquiver with all sizes, colours, and shapes of waterfowl. Now I discovered that the bag Sarah had sent along was stuffed with bread crusts and cake crumbs. When Harold instructed Fran and me to dispense largesse from it, we were mobbed by hundreds of swans, geese, and ducks yanking at our clothing with their beaks, flapping their wings, quacking, honking, and hissing. It was a bit like Alfred Hitchcock's eerie film, *The Birds*, except that it had no ominous overtones.

Most of these birds were exceedingly gentle even while taking food from our hands. The exception was an Egyptian gander who seized my fingers in his horny beak and would not let go. There ensued a tug-of-war that I lost on points. Peter was amused.

"Nasty chap, that one. Don't bend over or he'll go for your nose."

An Emperor goose crowded in behind Fran and vainly tried to get her attention by nibbling the hem of her skirt. When that failed the goose thrust her head and neck under the skirt, eliciting an instant response.

I was impressed by the avian display around us, but a little disapproving too, for I do not hold with keeping wild animals in captivity.

"It'd be better," I said in Fran's ear, "if all these birds were free to go where they pleased."

Peter overheard me. "Oh, but they *are*," he cried indignantly. "Look there!" He pointed towards the river flats where flight after flight of geese and ducks were rising and heading in our direction. Soon the air was throbbing and whistling with the sound of wings as flock after flock pitched into the mob surrounding us, anxious not to be too late for their "elevenses," as Maureen put it.

Leaving Maureen and Harold to deal with the swelling multitudes, Peter led Fran and me off to one side where we could hear ourselves think.

"There are about forty-odd species in the Big Pen at this moment," he told us. "Some are native to Britain, but most are rare types brought here from all over the world. And most *are* free to come and go as they please. Only the really endangered ones are pinioned, to make sure they don't come to any grief."

Peter himself had originally doubted the wisdom of allowing the foreign birds their freedom. Time reassured him. There had been only one serious "break" and it was unintentional.

A flock of snow geese, the nucleus of which Scott had brought back from arctic Canada, was in the habit of making a morning exercise flight over the Severn estuary. One January in 1952 a heavy fog swept in while the birds were aloft and they got lost.

The English being the nature lovers they are, a nationwide search ensued. The BBC broadcast special alerts. Bird watchers sallied out in their hundreds. Peter chartered a plane and flew up and down the coast, hoping to find the flock and shepherd it back to the Dumbles. A lone bird was reported a hundred miles to the north, wearily slogging its way on foot across a farmer's field. Others were seen in remote parts of the British Isles, but only half a dozen found their own way home. Peter thought the rest had probably been shot.

Those who returned were so shaken by the experience of life in the raw that thereafter they took to the air only on clear days and for brief periods.

I asked Peter if there had been much trouble with poachers.

"Not really. What I've done, you see, is give every known or suspected poacher for miles and miles around special warden membership in the Trust." He smiled. "Works like a charm. It'd be as much as a man's life was worth to take a shot at one of our birds now."

That happy breed of killers who call themselves sportsmen would have found the targets massed before us irresistible. The variety alone would have made them drool. In the milling mobs around Harold and Maureen, I could pick out black swans from Australia, trumpeter swans from Canada, Sushkin's geese from Siberia, half a dozen species of European geese, Bahamian pintails, Chilean teal, Abyssinian yellowbills, African pollards, New Zealand scaup, Brazilian teal, Magellan geese, and other species, as they say, too numerous to mention.

If the variety of world rarities would have driven a sport hunter half insane, the numbers would have ensured dementia.

Although it was summer, between two and three thousand geese and about twice as many ducks remained in the vicinity of the sanctuary, spreading out over the Dumbles to feed and breed. In winter, Peter told us, as many as ten thousand northern geese, mainly greylag, pink-footed, and white-fronted, ended their southerly migration flight on the Dumbles, where they remained until spring sent them back to Iceland and Greenland to raise new families.

Peter had begun his work with a lease on the land and not much else. His own small collection of live ducks and geese had vanished during the war years. He had no funds. But, as it turned out, he did have the support of a great many people who also realized that the sonorous voices crying on high in autumnal nights; the rush of wings over the marshes of the world; the kaleidoscopic play of living grace and colour on lakes, rivers, and ponds were fast fading away. These people rallied around him to organize the Severn Wild Fowl Trust. Founding members included Field Marshal Viscount Alanbrooke, His Excellency Ahmen Aboud Pasha, half a dozen lords of the realm, and, most important, several thousand ordinary Britons.

Help came from unexpected quarters. When the holding and breeding pens were being built, paths laid, and ponds dug, much of the labour was provided gratis by German prisoners of war who were awaiting repatriation in a nearby camp. They volunteered almost en masse.

"It was a jolly queer sight, you know; all those *Kriegsmarine*,

Luftwaffe, and *Wehrmacht* types rousting about in the mud, singing and larking like schoolboys to help a lot of birds. Why? I really can't say. We couldn't pay them anything. The foreman — he was a former paratrooper — told me once that just having a flock of greylags spiral down around him as if he was an old chum made him feel life might still be worth the living. He wanted to stay on permanently, but the authorities wouldn't let him."

As is all too often the case, the authorities gave Scott a lot of trouble. The hunting-shooting lobby in England wields great power, as indeed it does in every well-to-do country. It did not like Scott's application for the establishment of a no-hunting zone that would embrace much of the Dumbles. The lobby feared Scott would establish a dangerous precedent. Had the public not rallied strongly to his cause and won the day, the Trust would have found itself largely limited to rearing living targets for gunners, a fate that has overtaken all too many waterfowl "sanctuaries" in North America.

Then there was the Royal Air Force, which had several airfields in the region. In 1949 the RAF decided the Dumbles would make an excellent bombing and rocket-firing range. Expropriation proceedings were begun and would have succeeded had not the public become militantly aroused on behalf of Peter and the birds. Seldom defeated in the air, the RAF had to accept defeat on the ground. It did so with such bad grace that, when we were there, pilots of screaming jets were still going out of their way to "strafe" the geese.

"The odd thing is," said Peter with a grin, "the geese seem to know they've got the upper hand. I've often seen them casually break away in front of a jet like a bunch of children enjoying an exciting game. Or they'll sit unruffled on the flats and cackle with glee when a pilot diving on them has to pull up before he goes into the drink."

In the beginning the sanctuary harboured only about fifty waterfowl of ten species. By the end of the first year it held seventy different kinds. As word of Scott's intention to provide a breeding refuge for threatened species got around, a swelling stream of rare and endangered birds began arriving at Slimbridge. By 1952 the stream of refugees had become a feathered torrent flowing from every quarter of the globe, bringing such diverse creatures as flightless Steamer ducks from Tierra del Fuego; harlequin ducks from Labrador, pygmy geese from India, Koloa ducks from Hawaii, and Ross's geese from arctic Canada.

The most immediately threatened species constituted Peter's chief concern. These he set about rearing in the relative freedom, but security, of the sanctuary. He had two goals in mind. The first was to build a stock that would be large enough to ensure against total extinction if the species should disappear in the wild. The second was to rear additional birds to reinforce the wild stock in home territories where the species had been badly depleted.

Peter led the four of us to the rearing pens to meet a group of one of the rarest birds alive — the strikingly marked

Hawaiian Né Né. Two geese, one gander, and nine half-grown Né Né goslings noisily greeted us from their roomy enclosure, crowding up to the fence for a snack of Sar's cake crumbs. While they gabbled and gobbled, Peter told us their story.

Once abundant on the Hawaiian islands, the Né Né had, by 1945, been so reduced by gunners, introduced mongooses, and feral cats that none survived in the wild. Although a few still existed in captivity in Hawaii, they could not be induced to breed.

The species appeared doomed. Then, in 1952, with only forty Né Né left in existence, the Hawaiian authorities sent a pair to Slimbridge in the faint hope that Scott would have better luck.

Alas, Né Né cannot be easily told apart as to sex (at least not by human beings) and it turned out both geese *were* geese. A frantic exchange of radiograms resulted in a bona fide gander being airlifted halfway around the world. He arrived too late for the 1952 breeding season, but in 1953 fathered the nine lusty-looking goslings we saw before us.

"May not seem like very many but actually it's a terrific start," Peter said proudly. "If God is with us and with the geese, two or three years from now we'll be able to start sending some home to Hawaii to be released in a protected area where they can begin bringing their species back from the brink."[*]

---

[*]*Releases have been made and the Né Né is now out of immediate danger and becoming re-established in the wild.*

We congratulated him, but he was diffident. "Really, it's a very small success. There may be as many as two dozen kinds of waterfowl currently threatened with extinction; and even that's not the worst of it. All over the world, especially in the wealthy countries, hunters have knocked waterfowl populations into a cocked hat. I'm afraid we may have scores of threatened species by the end of the century. It's very nice to help the Né Né, but there's still the devil of a lot to be done."

Keeping the 130 different kinds of waterfowl gathered together at Slimbridge fed and in good health was a tremendous task, most of which fell on the shoulders of a young man named Sam Johnston. Young fish-eating ducks, for example, had to be started on a diet of maggots raised in the Trust's very own maggot factory. Older fish-eaters required vast quantities of small eels, sprats, and herring. Geese, fortunately, are mostly grass-eaters; but some geese and many sea ducks need marine plants, which Johnston and a crew of volunteers harvested in the estuary from a rickety old rowboat.

Another of Johnston's problems was keeping the various species of birds sorted out. Native waterfowl from all over Europe frequently dropped in, and some concluded this was the life for them and stayed for good. Some very rare birds, such as a Bewick's swan, arrived in this manner. These freeloaders, as Peter called them, sometimes mate with exotics from afar. The offspring quite literally look like nothing on earth. Weirdly marked hybrids wander happily about the pens and fly over the salt flats, making the job of record-keeping exceedingly difficult and giving amateur ornithologists conniptions. However, anything with wings was welcome at Slimbridge.

"I expect some scientists don't quite approve of how we do things," Peter apologized, "because, you see, we believe in everything being left as natural as possible. We try not to interfere more than we absolutely have to. Birds are like us, you know. If they feel at ease they do well. Otherwise they can go all to pieces."

He told us a story to illustrate this. Egyptian geese tend to be troublemakers so it was decided to send all except one gander away to a waterfowl park in Hampshire. The deprived gander thereupon fell madly in love with Johnston.

"It's the same nasty old bird that bit your hand. Used to follow poor Sam everywhere, trying to mate with him. Simply wouldn't take no for an answer. Poor chap was black-and-blue from fighting off the gander's advances. Then Sam got a bright idea. He shut the bird up in a shed with a German shepherd someone had given us for a watchdog . . . something we surely didn't need, not with several thousand geese about the place.

"Then, you see, the gander switched his affections to the dog. When Sam let them out, the poor shepherd was driven quite demented. Finally went to ground under the viewing stand where visitors go to watch the birds. Wouldn't come out at all. Just lay under there and howled as if his heart was breaking. Clearly either the gander or the dog had to go, and since the dog had no feathers, of course he was the one. We did find him a good home with an old chap in the village who can't abide birds. They get along famously, I'm told."

Peter and I got along famously too. Fran and the Shortts began to complain of hunger pangs and while they retired to the nearest pub for a bite of lunch, Peter took me for a walking tour of the Dumbles.

It carried me back to boyhood hikes looking for birds on the Saskatchewan prairie. Ducks and geese had still been abundant in those days but I had never expected to see them again in comparable numbers and variety. Walking (and wading) the Dumbles with Scott was like returning to another time. I did not keep count, but I am sure we saw a dozen kinds of geese and swans, and twice that many kinds of ducks.

All were fearless of us. Once when we perched on the edge of a seawall for a rest, a small flock of greylags came streaming across the estuary, saw us, veered abruptly, and pitched into the salt grass within arm's length. Straining their necks, they gurgled at us pleadingly.

"Young ganders," Peter apologized. "Should have gone off to Iceland in the spring with the rest of their lot. Now they seem to think it's up to me to find mates for them."

Farther along was a concrete pillbox built during the war to house a machine gun, as part of Britain's coastal defences. Peter had converted it into an observation blind. We spent an hour in it munching apples he pulled from a jacket pocket, smoking our pipes, and enjoying the show the birds were staging over the salt marshes and tidal flats.

The thought came to me that, although the need for sanctuary may be more immediate and urgent for some than for others, *all* creatures need it at some juncture in their lives. *All* creatures, including us.

I wanted to put the thought into words but felt awkward about doing so. Instead, I chose to remark on the concrete box through whose gun embrasures we were watching the birds.

"Hell of a good idea, this. Turning the sword into the ploughshare, as it were."

Peter nodded. "Wouldn't it be grand to do the same with all the military hardware in the world?"

"Too bloody true! Only I'm afraid that isn't going to happen."

As if to emphasize the point, three Meteor jet fighters shrieked low overhead. I flinched, but the ducks and geese on the Dumbles paid no heed. They were in sanctuary.

A pair of lapwings mewed past, flapping their wings like giant bats. Peter watched them intently.

"P'raps you're right. It may *not* come to pass . . . but you know, Mowat, if it doesn't . . . and if we don't stop mucking things up other ways as well . . . one day the old Proprietor up in the sky is going to shout: 'Time, gentlemen!' and turn the lot of us out into the night."

His voice sank almost to a whisper, taking on the cadence of a childhood verse.

"And where will we go then, poor things? . . . And where will we go then? . . ."

ABOUT THE AUTHOR

FARLEY MOWAT, author of such distinguished books as *Never Cry Wolf, A Whale for the Killing, Sea of Slaughter,* and most recently, *Born Naked,* has long been eloquent in his indictment of man's exploitation of both human and non-human life. He was born in Trenton, Ontario in 1921 and began writing in 1949 after serving in the Second World War and subsequently spending two years in the Arctic. More than 14 million copies of Farley Mowat's many books have sold worldwide and he has been published in 52 languages. Farley Mowat lives in Port Hope, Ontario, and River Bourgeois, Nova Scotia with his wife, writer Claire Mowat.